AN INTRODUCTION TO THE

POLITICS
OF THE
INDONESIAN
UNION
MOVEMENT

The **ISEAS – Yusof Ishak Institute** (formerly Institute of Southeast Asian Studies) is an autonomous organization established in 1968. It is a regional centre dedicated to the study of socio-political, security, and economic trends and developments in Southeast Asia and its wider geostrategic and economic environment. The Institute's research programmes are grouped under Regional Economic Studies (RES), Regional Strategic and Political Studies (RSPS), and Regional Social and Cultural Studies (RSCS). The Institute is also home to the ASEAN Studies Centre (ASC), the Nalanda-Sriwijaya Centre (NSC), and the Singapore APEC Study Centre.

ISEAS Publishing, an established academic press, has issued more than two thousand books and journals. It is the largest scholarly publisher of research about Southeast Asia from within the region. ISEAS Publishing works with many other academic and trade publishers and distributors to disseminate important research and analyses from and about Southeast Asia to the rest of the world.

AN INTRODUCTION TO THE

POLITICS
OF THE
INDONESIAN
UNION
MOVEMENT

MAX LANE

ISEAS YUSOF ISHAK
INSTITUTE

First published in Singapore in 2019 by
ISEAS Publishing
30 Heng Mui Keng Terrace
Singapore 119614

Email: publish@iseas.edu.sg
Website: <http://bookshop.iseas.edu.sg>

The responsibility for facts and opinions in this publication rests exclusively with the author and his interpretations do not necessarily reflect the views or the policy of the publisher or its supporters.

ISEAS Library Cataloguing-in-Publication Data

Names: Lane, Max, 1951–
Title: An Introduction to the Politics of the Indonesian Union
 Movement / Max Lane.
Description: Singapore : ISEAS – Yusof Ishak Institute, 2019. | Includes
 bibliographical references.
Identifiers: ISBN 9789814843300 (paperback) | ISBN 978-981-4843-31-7
 (pdf) | ISBN 978-981-4843-52-2 (epub)
Subjects: LCSH: Labor unions--Political activity--Indonesia. | Labor
 movement--Political aspects--Indonesia. | Indonesia--Politics and
 government.
Classification: LCC HD6823.5 L26

Typeset by Superskill Graphics Pte Ltd

Contents

Preface: Introducing an Overview of Trade Union Politics

This essay introduces the basic, visible politics of the Indonesian trade union movement, with a focus on the period 2010–14. To provide this introduction clearly, it also presents an overview of the politics of trade unions before the end of the New Order and the legacies from the New Order, which constitutes the terrain of the current situation. Indonesia has experienced two major upheavals affecting trade unions, in 1965 and in 1998. It is impossible to understand current trade union politics without understanding those events and their legacies.

To provide this overview, I have primarily relied on documentary sources. Where possible, I have given references to English language material. To assist understanding of some developments, I have quoted at length from interviews, statements and articles by union figures, translating or using available translations. These include newspaper reports, material produced by union and activist groups and studies by commentators and academics. During the last twenty-five years, in the course of writing on Indonesian politics, I have also established communications with a range of people active in the union movement, most of them on the left of the political spectrum. I have been careful to refer to official publications of unions with which I have had no personal contact as well as to their statements to the media.

One argument I present here is that the emergence of trade unions after 1998 is a process still at its beginning. Even at the beginning of this process, there are more than fourteen trade union confederations, scores of federations, and probably thousands of new, or renewed, workplace unions. Many are registered only at the provincial or district level. It is impossible at this point to know exactly what is happening among the leaderships or memberships of these many unions. This essay concentrates on an overview of union activity that is visible as a factor on the national political stage. This means concentrating on unions whose memberships are probably a minority of the total union membership and an even smaller minority of the total workforce. This minority, through highly organized activity, has made a visible impact on both labour politics and national politics. This essay does not, therefore, pretend to be able to provide a comprehensive picture of the political life of the three million or more people who are union members, but rather an introduction to those union activities most visible in national politics.

There is a small body of literature that developed on labour politics in Indonesia since 1998. Most of these studies are very much case-study focused. Probably the most important book on the post 2010 period is the collection of articles in *Kebangkitan Gerakan Buruh: Refleksi Era Reformasi* edited by Jafar Suryomenggolo. The several contributors to this book are also actors in the labour scene, of one kind or another. These essays are also primarily case studies. There has been no attempt to provide an overview of the evolution of the trade union sector as a whole, nor of trade union roles in mainstream politics. Given the new, fluid and fragmented nature of the development of trade unions and labour politics, this is understandable. This attempt to provide such an overview of at least the political activity of trade unions is also challenged by this newness, fluidity and fragmentation. It should be seen as an initial introductory essay. The size and the fragmentation of the subject matter, and the unevenness in the documentary material produced by the labour movement itself, mean that available data is also uneven and sometimes has an anecdotal character. However, I believe this introduction to the overall terrain will be a useful starting point for further observation, even as the labour sector further evolves and changes.

In trying to understand the developments introduced here, we need to approach the subject fully cognisant of the great difference between labour union politics in Indonesia and either in the advanced industrial countries or in developing countries where there has been prolonged periods of democratic space allowing trade union activity. Indonesia is both an under-industrialized country, where most manufacturing that does exist is relatively new, and which went for a period of more than thirty years without any real democratic space for trade union organizing. When approaching the experience of other countries, we can assume accumulated experience (traditions), accumulated organization loyalties and simplification and amalgamations, not fragmentation. Grasping the newness, the early stage of development after a long period of virtual non-existence, is crucial to understanding what is happening and the constraints on observation and analysis.

Chapter 1

The Legacy of State Authoritarian Unionism

The number and diversity of trade unions has more than simply increased dramatically since the fall of Suharto in 1998. The union terrain has been completely reshaped. At the same time, it should be noted from the outset that the percentage of the workforce actually organized in unions remains minuscule. The Indonesian workforce is usually assessed at around 150 million people—more if child workers of one kind or another are included. There are various figures for union membership, but it is unlikely that it would reach 5 million or 3 per cent of the workforce,[1] and is likely much less than that. Indonesian society remains fundamentally unindustrialized. Petty commodity production of one kind or another dominates in the provision of both goods and services. Perhaps more than 90 per cent of workplaces have fewer than 20 employees,[2] and are mostly unorganizable in the current atmosphere.

This still means, however, that there are between 5 and 10 million people—probably closer to 5 than to 10—working in enterprises with a big enough workforce to make their unionization practical in a situation of their being only a limited number of experienced union organizers. According to 2016 Ministry of Manpower data, there are now 14 trade union confederations, 112 federations and at least 7,000 workplace unions.[3] Some unions are registered, for at least some of the time, with the Ministry of Manpower; some have local registration.

It would not be inappropriate to say that unions mushroomed in their thousands since the fall of Suharto, but neither would such a statement provide a true picture of what has happened since May 1998. The 2016 Ministry of Manpower statistics cite a total union membership of just over 2.7 million. We can assume that this figure is based on membership size claimed by registered unions, there being no way to check the reality of active membership. Furthermore, these 2.7 million members are divided among at least 112 federations.

There are also many other limitations flowing from both the sociological and socio-economic situation and from the country's political history. The political legacy from before 1998 both sets the framework for the trade union sector today and has helped to form the leadership terrain. This framework and its intersection with contemporary social and economic reality are full of contradictions and thus have the potential for development in more than one direction, including the potential for the growth of a strong and militant movement, although that is not the current trend.

The framework for the contemporary trade union sector is a product of both the trade union system that existed under the New Order and the way that structure was ended. There are different aspects of this framework. One relates to the organizational legacies—that is, the organizations inherited by the post-1998 union world. Another, in some ways with deeper implications, is the experiential legacy: the knowledge and skills related to union and worker struggle accumulated within the working class. A third, also with deep implications, is the political and ideological legacies that frame workers' thinking about their bargaining and political power—their class consciousness.

Understanding the current dynamics and future direction of trade union politics is impossible without understanding these legacies. In many ways, it is the continuity with the past, not in a linear sense but in the form of dealing with the contradictions it has produced, that most determines contemporary dynamics. This legacy frames how political actors connected with the union sector respond to contemporary developments. The present has not yet assumed sovereignty of initiative over these legacies.

Pre-emptive Seizure of State Power

The establishment of the New Order was a seizure of power from the pre-existing government as a move to pre-empt the formation of a coalition government between the Indonesian Communist Party (PKI), Sukarno and other radical left forces. The pretext was a midnight conspiratorial mutiny by left-leaning army officers to remove the existing army leadership in order to open up more room to manoeuvre for the left in general. The conspiracy was badly implemented and foundered in several steps, including being unable to present detained generals to Sukarno for him to dismiss and being unable to neutralize the Army's Strategic Command, which was under the command of Major General Suharto. As the mutiny started to collapse, orders were given for the execution of several generals whom the mutineers had detained. On news of this, Sukarno made it clear he did not support the mutineers. The 30th September Movement, as they called themselves, failed. The newspaper of the PKI supported the left-leaning officers, which made it easier for Suharto and his allies to implicate the PKI. The executions of the generals were reported as happening after the generals were tortured, including having their genitals sliced by communist women, who first participated in sexual dances. These reports were totally untrue but were widely reported on the radio and in those newspapers still allowed to publish.[4]

The seizure of power by Suharto was integrated with a massive anti-left purge of society, involving systematic mass murder and the suppression of all left-wing activity and ideology. Hundreds of thousands of people were executed, tens of thousands imprisoned, and myriads of organizations banned or suspended.[5]

Among those killed and imprisoned were trade union leaders and members. Trade unions associated with the left were banned, including the biggest, Serikat Organisasi Buruh Seluruh Indonesia (SOBSI—All-Indonesia Union of Worker Organizations), which was connected to the PKI. All trade union activity was suspended, including by anti-communist trade unions, such as Islamic trade unions. Among the ideas most severely suppressed were those that emphasized class struggle and class identity. Over the first few years after 1965, the whole vocabulary of political discourse regarding class was replaced with a new one that attempted to eliminate all sense of conflict between classes. The historically used word for worker—*buruh*, connected with both anti-colonial and anti-capitalist struggle—was replaced with the word *karyawan*, meaning someone who exerts effort, or *pekerja*, someone who works.[6] Neither term carried a strong connection with the history of trade union struggle.

These events took place in the situation of a total suppression of the left in general, widespread use of terror, and a radical ideological reorientation of the whole country away from left and socialist ideas and in support of capitalist development through integration with the world economy, organized in cooperation with the governments of the developed world.

Authoritarian State Unionism[7]

Under the New Order (1965–98), the state, through the government and its ministries as well as through the armed forces, enforced a single trade union structure—at first in the form of a federation, then a single national union and finally a new federated structure—under state domination. Both the state and its union were opposed to and eschewed any sharpening of open class tensions. This policy of Major General Suharto began to be implemented as early as October 1965.

Between 1965 and 1972, there was no trade union activity at all. A union body was established in 1968. Its activities were very little, apart from recruiting people who could staff the structure of a state-sponsored union, the Federasi Buruh Seluruh Indonesia (FBSI—All-Indonesia Workers Federation), which was founded a few years later. In accordance with the policy on vocabulary, this was later changed to the Serikat Pekerja Seluruh Indonesia (SPSI—All-Indonesia Workers Union).

Between 1965 and 1998, there was a single trade union ideology, focused on partnership between *karyawan* and entrepreneurs and hostile to any employee-employer conflict. From the late 1960s until 1997, only one trade union federation was allowed, staffed in large part—though not totally—by military and company personnel.[8] This was initially a federation of theoretically independent sectoral industrial unions, but was later replaced with a unified, centralized structure, which had industrial sections rather than separate unions. It was then later re-federated, but only after the unitary streamlining had been implemented.

Authoritarian state unionism as a form of totalitarian management of trade unions and industrial relations lasted,

more or less unchallenged, for 33 years out of the 48 years of
independent Indonesia's peacetime existence. These 33 years had
followed 15 years (1950–65) of intense contestation in which
no specific mode of union organization had been stabilized and
consolidated. The New Order legacy to the period after 1998 has,
therefore, been fundamental, imposing for the first time a stable
mode of union organization—but with contradictory impacts.

Organizational Legacy

The New Order created a single centralized structure for all trade
union activity, the Federasi Serikat Pekerja Seluruh Indonesia
(FSPSI—Federation of Indonesian Trade Unions).[9] This structure
was used to keep industrial conflict at a minimum, and exerted
very effective control over the workforce for most of the time
and in most places, but it also had major inherent weaknesses,
which would become very obvious after the fall of the New Order.
Most fundamentally, the strength and authority of the union
leadership came from the fact that it was backed by the full force
of the state, rather than the support of an active membership.
The state ensured its finances (although unions also collected
dues via employers), many personnel were assigned from the
military, and, crucially, neither the union as an institution nor its
leaders ever faced any competition from alternative institutions or
leaderships. It was a creature of the state and dependent on it.[10]

   At the same time, it is important to consider the implications
of the fact that the FBSI/SPSI undertook this role during more than
a quarter of a century in which large-scale enterprises expanded
rapidly in Indonesia, compared to what had existed before
1965. Significant foreign investment and income generated from
that—followed in the mid-1970s by a very substantial increase in
government revenue from oil exports—meant that the number

of factories increased, so that workplaces that needed to be organized also increased significantly. There were also state-run enterprises or sectors in which industrial relations needed to be managed, in electricity generation, railways, harbours, airports and plantations, as well as professions such as teachers. This remained a tiny percentage of the workforce, but represented a major challenge to the kind of organization that the FBSI/SPSI was. Even in its role as co-manager (with the state) of industrial peace, there was an increasing number of technical activities it needed to undertake under various industrial relations laws. These included concluding collective bargaining agreements as well as participating in various tripartite structures with government and business. While not actually providing freedom of organization, as required by international conventions, the Indonesian government did mimic many aspects of internationally accepted formal industrial relations practices.

Moreover, in the 1980s there was a very substantial increase in worker protests, often initiated outside union structures. These waves of protest continued for several years and were widely reported in the media.[11] This represented a further challenge to the FBSI/SPSI to channel this activity with less conflict, although the repressive wing of the state was also used.

This meant that an increasing percentage of the staff of the FBSI/SPSI needed to become "trade union professionals" to keep the wheels of the organization turning. There appears to be no research data on the recruitment sources of union officials during the second half of the SPSI's existence, 1980–98. In the earlier period, most analysts concluded that the institution drew on military personnel and, at the factory level, sometimes the staff of the enterprise. At the same time, it is also clear that in the early stage the FBSI absorbed people who had been active in non-left trade unions before 1965 or from one ally of the New

Order that included an element that did believe in trade unions on the traditional social democratic model. The first chairperson of the FBSI in 1973 was Agus Sudono, a leader of the Association of Indonesian Islamic Trade Unions (GSBII—Gabungan Serikat Buruh Islam Indonesia) from before 1965.[12] Others were recruited from similar organizations. There were also people recruited from the Partai Sosialis Indonesia (PSI—Indonesian Socialist Party). The PSI, a small social democratic party, was banned by Sukarno as a result of its opposition to him and the PKI. Some of its intellectuals aligned themselves with General Suharto's new government. However, it also had a wing that could be characterized as left-of-centre social democrats, some of whom had histories in the union sector before 1965.[13] Some of these people were also recruited. Some also came from the student organization affiliated to the PSI, Gerakan Mahasiswa Sosialis (GEMSOS—Socialist Students Movement). This included Haruno, who became the central leader of a key sectoral union in the early period, the Serikat Buruh Logam dan Keramik (SBLK—Ceramic and Metal Workers' Union).[14]

There are indications that these kinds of people acted as recruiters into the 1980s and 1990s, drawing in a new layer of professional trade unionists but increasingly without the same ideological or political experience as the first generation.[15] New political experience was accumulated in the terrain of state authoritarianism, including integration into the state party, GOLKAR, or one of the other two permitted parties,[16] and collective bargaining agreements between *karyawan* and employers as "partners".

The SPSI faced the post-authoritarian environment without state backing and without the experience of either operating without state backing or in a competitive environment. Only a section of its personnel were part of the experienced trade union apparatus, some of whom were drawn from Islamic and social democratic political lineages, and some more integrated into New Order political institutions, including those that survived the collapse of the New Order, such as GOLKAR.

Apart from the organizational legacy of *state authoritarian unionism*—namely a state-supported single union structure—it is also necessary to look at the legacy left by pre-1998 dissident union organizations. Most of these developed after 1990.

Legacy of Dissident Union Organization

Dissident union organizations emerged in the 1990s outside of, and as a rejection of, the SPSI—indeed in opposition to the New Order altogether. There had been dissident activity in the early 1980s, when the SBLK, under the leadership of Haruno, offered resistance to the New Order's general authoritarianism and to its tight hands-on control over the affairs of sectoral unions. SBLK leaders voiced their criticism in FBSI congresses and also in their own newspaper *Dinamka* (1980–81), until it was ordered stopped. Any serious assertion of sectoral union independence was undermined by the dissolution of the federation structure and the formation of the SPSI. The next wave of organized dissidence occurred in 1991. Labour dissidence during the 1990s also helped shape the contemporary union terrain in crucial ways, providing the basis for a distinctive stream in union organizing up until today.

Serikat Buruh Merdeka Setia Kawan (SBM-SK) and Serikat Buruh Sejahtera Indonesia (SBSI)

The first initiative was the formation of Serikat Buruh Merdeka Setia Kawan (SBM-SK—Solidarity Trade Union) in September 1990. The organization was established by figures very much within the original New Order ideological realm, but from among those who had become disenchanted. The president of the union was Ponke Princen, an Indonesian citizen of Dutch descent and an opponent of the PKI and Sukarno before 1965. Princen had been detained under Sukarno. He later became a critic of Suharto's authoritarianism.[17] Others included a former official of the FBSI/SPSI, Saut Aritonang, whose contacts in the workplace were important. Another key figure was Muchtar Pakpahan, who later went on to start another union, the Serikat Buruh Sejahtera Indonesia (SBSI—Indonesia Prosperity Trade Union). The SBM-SK was harassed, but not banned, by the government and quickly collapsed under the pressure of internal contradictions. The primary contradiction was that between Aritonang, coming from an SPSI background, and Princen and others, who looked at the New Order situation in broader political terms.

SBSI was formed in 1992, shortly after SBM-SK collapsed. It modelled itself on what it saw as the orthodox "social democratic" unions in Europe. It had some connections with Christian Democratic political parties and unions in Europe. It incorporated some members who had been previously cultivated by non-union labour advocacy groups. It moved quickly to take industrial action, but its president, the lawyer Muchtar Pakpahan, was arrested in 1994 and again in 1996. Despite his arrest, SBSI continued to exist. It should be noted that while SBSI's industrial campaigning had an important political character insofar as campaigning constituted an act of defiance against New Order authoritarianism and thus encouraged pro-democratic activity, SBSI's ideological outlook did not see unions as more than mechanisms for bargaining over immediate wages and conditions and general welfare. After 1998, Pakpahan launched a labour party as a separate mechanism, but the SBSI's base did not have a sufficient mass to make any headway in growing support for the party.

In terms of legacy, the SBM-SK was not around long enough to have an impact. The SBSI, on the other hand, continues today. Crucially, its "social democratic" outlook has meant that it has come to represent a minor, though not insignificant, competing element within the majority trade union current today, mostly comprising the "descendants" of the SPSI.

Pusat Perjuangan Buruh Indonesia (PPBI)

The Pusat Perjuangan Buruh Indonesia (PPBI—Indonesian Centre for Labour Struggles) was formed in October 1994 as an initiative of ideologically left-wing elements, mainly students, who also launched the People's Democratic Union in 1994, the People's Democratic Party (PRD—Partai Rakyat Demokratik) in 1996,[18] the Indonesian Students in Solidarity with Democracy (SMID—Solidaritas Mahasiswa Indonesia untuk Demokrasi), the National Peasants Union (STN—Serikat Tani Nasional) and the Cultural Work Network (Jaker—Jaringan Kerja Kebudayaan). This network of activists had been organizing through other groups in the few years before 1994. Their ideological orientation set different campaign frameworks than for the SBSI, for both the long and short terms. Their long-term goal was a socialist Indonesia, which they saw as the only framework in which the welfare of workers, and the rest of the poor majority, could be advanced significantly. Their short-term goal was to end the authoritarian regime and so open up the democratic space in which labour politics, including the advocacy of socialism, would have more freedom. The fall of the New Order and winning the maximum democratic space for the working population's political activities was the immediate central goal. This contrasted markedly with the ideological orientation and strategic orientation of SBSI, which was willing to defy the New Order but whose political outlook was not aimed at overthrowing it, let alone overthrowing capitalism.

This gave the PPBI very different characteristics than the SBSI. As its name implied, its leaders saw it as a centre for struggle rather than as a "union" as such. Ongoing militant mobilizations around immediate demands related to wages and conditions were combined with a campaign for democratization, including an end to the military's role in politics and its direct protection of employers. These activities were coordinated with others of the above groups, especially SMID. The PRD itself was formed by the core of the network to play a similar role of helping to lead mobilization and radicalization against authoritarian rule (that is, a willingness to commit to high-risk organizing).

Through the PPBI, this network was able to organize very large strikes between 1993 and 1994, all of which gained high levels of press coverage. In addition to these very large strikes, there was ongoing strike and protest activity in several cities.[19] While these mobilizations were usually around wages and conditions or the right to organize, their political impact, and that of their press coverage and other publicity, played an important role in popularizing the idea of mobilization against the government. The uncompromising analysis and rhetoric put forward by the PPBI-SMID-PRD network helped create an atmosphere of increasingly militant opposition, which was their aim. Their outlook was not more political than the SBSI's but had different content. The latter was willing to act in defiance of the regime in a specific wages and conditions framework, while the former had a clear view of what kind of political change workers and the majority of the population needed. This was eventually socialism, and more immediately full democracy.

One key legacy therefore was in relation to ideology and political outlook, establishing a current of militant workers organizing and mobilizing behind radical political as well as economic goals. There was also an organizing culture. Organizing in either SBSI or PPBI entailed risks. However, the left ideology, political mass mobilizing and militancy sought by the PPBI-PRD-SMID network meant both greater risks and a different kind of engagement with workers at the grass roots. The PPBI network produced a generation of committed organizers capable of and willing to live with the masses. Working under difficult political conditions and with limited material resources also required tight organization and constant political education. This network therefore had two layers; namely, a public spokesperson layer and a non-public leadership and activist force. In the case of the PPBI, its chairperson, Dita Sari, was the central public spokesperson, while others, such as organizers Asep Salmin and Agus "Bobo", remained low profile. This practice existed across the whole PRD-SMID-PPBI network. It meant that when the PPBI and the PRD were banned and Dita Sari and other well-known public figures, such as Budiman Sujatmiko, were arrested, the majority of the central leadership, such as Danial Indrakusuma, Web Warouw and Asep Salmin, were able to remain free.[20]

The ability of the leadership structure to maintain itself throughout the 1990s up until 1998 meant the mobilizing and radicalization process was able to continue. This included the expansion of the number of activists in the labour sector. This had three impacts post-1998, which will be discussed in the next section. **First**, it meant that there was a structure to mobilize large numbers of workers, even though not under a union banner, in mass protests against the New Order during 1996–98. **Second**, it meant that there were the resources, an organized base and momentum for significant worker mobilizations in the months immediately after the fall of Suharto, establishing the atmosphere for a radical current of trade unions to start. **Third**, it meant there were cadre resources available for the establishment of such a current. Even in the post-2010 period, key central leaders or organizers in several non-SPSI unions can trace their origins back to the PPBI, especially its non-public cadres. This is true across the majority of left-oriented worker and activist groups, even in 2017, although aging and leadership regeneration have changed the balance. Unions that emerged in the 2000s that had former PPBI leaders and organizers in their leadership teams included the reconstituted PPBI, as the FNPBI; then later the Kongres Aliansi Serikat Buruh Indonesia[21] (KASBI—Congress of Indonesian Trade Union Alliances), initially connected to the Partai Rakyat Pekerja (PRP—Working People's Party, where ex-PRD activists played a key role); as well as today in union federations such as Federasi Serikat Buruh Demokratik Kerakyatan (F-SEDAR—Popular Democratic Workers' Union), Sentral Gerakan Buruh Nasional (SGBN—National Workers' Movement Center)[22] and Federasi Buruh Lintas Pabrik (FBLP—Cross-Factory Workers' Federation).[23] Other ideologically left union groups have emerged as part of a process that was possible because of the PPBI legacy, while adopting a different strain of left ideology.

Summing Up the Pre-1998 Legacies

The most easily identifiable legacies are those represented by organizations. Today's two largest trade union confederations are direct descendants of the SPSI—namely the Konfederasi Serikat Pekerja Seluruh Indonesia (KSPSI—Confederation of All Indonesia Trade Unions) and the Konfederasi Serikat Pekerja Indonesia (KPSI—Confederation of Indonesian Trade Unions). Some unions representing workers in state-owned enterprises have the same origin.

The legacy of the dissident unions is also significant. The SBSI still is of a significant size (despite having also split). Two other confederations, KASBI and the recently formed Konfederasi Persatuan Buruh Indonesia (KPBI—Indonesian Workers' Union Confederation), can both trace their origins to the PPBI dissident current. Furthermore, several federations can also be traced to this current. Of course, the very fact that there are several different descendants of the pre-1998 organization and currents indicates that they are not simply a mechanical reproduction of earlier organizations with minor adjustments to the times. The differences among them represent either different political or ideological outlooks or the different strategic and tactical perspectives that have evolved.

Their history can be understood properly only by also grasping the meaning of some of the deeper aspects of the legacies from before 1998. The structures that suddenly faced a new situation after May 1998 all had very specific underlying characteristics, which have been mentioned earlier.

In the case of the FBSI/SPSI, one of the most fundamental characteristics was the reliance on *state backing for leaderships*. There had been no open and democratic contestation for leadership within the SPSI, at either the national or sectoral levels. The relationship of leadership to membership was not mediated by real elections with either competing ideological outlooks or competing platforms. What "competition" may have taken place was in the form of lobbying for support within the government. Relations with cabinet ministers and with GOLKAR, the government political party, or with either of the other two permitted parties, the Islamic PPP (Partai Persatuan Pembangunan—United Development Party) or the "nationalist" PDI (Partai Demokrasi Indonesia—Indonesian Democratic Party), were more important than popular support among members.

Leaders looked upwards for support and downwards to manage the memberships.

Management of those below did, however, require successful completion of specific formal tasks such as collective bargaining agreements, collection of dues and so on. This meant that some "organic" relationships did exist, especially between the full-time functionaries of the sectoral (and therefore factory) unions. The SPSI was not a paper organization, but rather a worker management organization with a narrow and conservative agenda and a state-dependent leadership. A key result of this dependency has been either *shallow factory-level loyalties to particular unions* or *a long period of passivity which militates against members confronting existing leaderships* during this period and immediately afterwards.

The SBSI's own agenda was a traditional "social democratic" agenda of improvements to wages and conditions achieved through collective bargaining. It was, however, more willing to engage in strike activity—at least in its early period—when negotiations failed. It differed with the SPSI on this only in degree. *However, it was fundamentally different to the SPSI in the relationship between leadership and membership.* There was never any state support for SBSI's leaders; indeed, Pakpahan was jailed by the New Order. Loyalty from the membership had to be won from the beginning, whether for the leadership as a whole or for different segments of it. There was no tradition of "looking upwards" for support or backing, to the government or to elite political players.

This latter characteristic was also very much a feature of the PPBI current. Its whole existence as a struggle centre, espousing a pro-socialist ideology, put it in confrontation with those above. Dealings with dissident elements within the elite were done as independent providers of critical support, putting demands upon them for more radical action.[24] The PPBI, however, produced a more complex ideological legacy. This had several components. There was an ideological commitment to a method of struggle: mass mobilization—*aksi massa*. There was an ideological struggle to win full democracy, which required an end to all restrictions on political organization and advocacy. Furthermore, the current had an ideological critique hostile to capitalism and to the foreign capitalist domination (imperialism) of Indonesia. In the 1990s, the concrete focus of its efforts was on ending the dictatorship, the withdrawal of the army from politics (i.e., an end to repressive activity), and general political liberalization.

In the last phase of the struggle against the New Order, this current advocated forming people's councils wherever the popular mobilization was big enough to do so. The rapid desertion of Suharto by his elite and Suharto's resignation as the mobilizations grew was, however, a sufficient victory to demobilize a majority of students and others. The mobilizations did not have the chance to escalate. Elite figures, including those who had joined the critical chorus against Suharto in late 1997 and early 1998, spoke out against the people's council idea, labelling it communist. But, in any case, the movement did not reach that level.

The ideological legacy of militant, radical democratic politics was to face a new situation once the New Order had collapsed and more democratic space opened up. The new situation was also an interesting new framework for the organizational aspects of the PPBI-PRD-SMID current. To what extent in a demobilized atmosphere would a "struggle centre" still work compared to a traditional union structure? To what extent would an ideologically aligned workers' organization be effective, especially one aligned to the left?

At the same time, there was a small layer of full-time and hardened and still ideological field organizers and leaders who survived the New Order.

Union Members' Experience

There is another aspect of the above history that also requires consideration. This relates to the kind of experience that union members underwent and accumulated. Although the question of how workers' experience during the 1990s affects today's terrain is mediated by the twenty years since 1998 during which new workers have entered the workforce, the experience of the 1990s has provided the foundations and even determined in a fundamental way some, if not all, aspects of the new generation's experience.

The key factor is that the majority of workers in unions or in workplaces during the 1990s gained almost no experience at all of union organizing, of being an actual member of a trade union.[25] *As a result, they have had no experience to pass on to the next generations, except of passivity.* This situation will have been worsened by the fact that the 1997 Asian financial crisis hit Indonesia hard, with tens of thousands of workers losing their jobs. What political or organizing experience some of them may have had was lost to future workers, as those who had lost their jobs moved into the informal sector or returned to the village. Factory work opportunities started to grow again only after 2000, requiring the recruitment of new young workers from villages and small towns who had even less experience of union life—usually zero.[26]

Union membership under state authoritarian unionism required almost no activity on the part of the majority of workers. Strikes through the union were almost non-existent. What strikes there were, for example in the 1980s, were outside union structures and without means of institutionalizing the memory of the experience. Of course, a layer of workers were integrated into structures needed for the completion of collective bargaining agreements and so on, but these were very small in number and were required to be active at only the most minimal level, and more as administrators rather than field organizers of industrial campaigning. Despite the practical tasks it had to complete, the SPSI was still essentially a manager of industrial relations, not an organization that represented workers, let alone organized them. The Indonesian working class, for thirty-three years, was without any experience of meaningful participation in either representational or struggle organizations. This only makes more shallow and fragile any sense of loyalty between membership and the union and its leadership.

In terms of the SPSI legacy, therefore, it is important to conceive of a situation in which the leadership has had no accountability to those below, only to those above in the state, and the membership has had no real organizational experience for several generations. Once the leaderships lost state backing and had to look for support from members, the situation would be ripe for splits, fragmentation and regrouping, as well as the emergence of new leaders. There would also be the evolution of new ways to "look above" for support.

Notes

1. One official figure gives a total of only 2.7 million members. Organisasi Pekerja/Buruh Di Indonesia Menurut Provinsi Tahun 2016 data obtained from Ministry of Manpower by AMR, Hong Kong.
2. See Daniel Bellefleur, Zahra Murad and Patrick Tangkau, "A Snapshot of Indonesian Entrepreneurship and Micro, Small, and Medium Sized Enterprise Development", US AID, https://crawford.anu.edu.au/acde/ip/pdf/lpem/2012/20120507-SMERU-Dan-Thomson-Bellefleur.pdf.
3. Organisasi Pekerja/Buruh Di Indonesia Menurut Provinsi Tahun 2016 data obtained from Ministry of Manpower by AMR, Hong Kong. A complete list of the names of all confederations does not seem to be available.

4. There are several researched academic works on the events of 30 September 1965. The brief summary here is primarily based on the latest research by John Roosa, *Pretext for Mass Murder: The September 30th Movement and Suharto's Coup d'État in Indonesia* (University of Wisconsin Press, 2006).

5. For an outline analysis of what I have called a counter-revolution, see Max Lane, *Unfinished Nation: Indonesia before and after Suharto* (Verso, 2008).

6. Jaques Leclerc, "An Ideological Problem of Indonesian Trade Unionism in the Sixties: 'Karyawan' versus 'Buruh'", *Review of Indonesian and Malayan Studies* 6, no. 1 (1972): 76–91.

7. This terminology for the form of unionism existing under the New Order is taken from Rob Lambert, *Authoritarian State Unionism in New Order Indonesia* (Asia Research Centre, Murdoch University, 1993).

8. Ibid.

9. While regulations in 1994 did allow enterprise unions outside the FSPSI to be formed, in practice this was discouraged. Unions were also formally banned from forming a rival federation. Michele Ford, "Continuity and Change in Indonesian Labour Relations in the Habibie Interregnum", *Southeast Asian Journal of Social Science* 28, no. 2 (2000): 67.

10. For another perspective of the legacy of institutional design, see T.L. Caraway, "Protective Repression, International Pressure, and Institutional Design: Explaining Labor Reform in Indonesia", *Studies in Comparative International Development* 39, no. 3 (2004): 28–49.

11. See the Clipping Service available in Menzies Library, Australian National University, a collection of Indonesian newspaper reports on labour and peasant activities during the 1980s; see also INDOC, *Workers Right to Organise* (Leiden, 1986); see also Max Lane, "Worker Resistance to Exploitation in Indonesia, 1981–82", *Newsletter of International Labour Studies* no. 18 (1983).

Published book length works on Indonesian trade unions during different periods between 1965 and 1998 include Vedi Hadiz, *Workers and the State in New Order Indonesia* (Routledge, 1997) and Michele

Ford, *Workers and Intellectuals: NGOs, Trade Unions and the Indonesian Labour Movement* (Singapore: National University of Singapore Press/ Hawai'i University Press/KITLV, 2009).

12. This union was formed on the initiative of Partai Majelis Syuro Muslimin Indonesia (MASYUMI—Party of the Council of Indonesian Muslim Associations) in 1947. Masyumi was a long-term opponent of the PKI and was banned by Sukarno in 1960, although its membership and affiliated organizations continued to be active. See Agus Sudono, *FBSI dahulu, sekarang dan yang akan datang* (Jakarta: FBSI, 1983).

13. During 1980–81, I regularly visited this grouping's offices.

14. During 1980–81, I regularly visited the SBLK offices in the garage of a house in Jalan Diponegoro, Menteng. For more on SBLK, see the newspaper *Dinamika*, available at the Menzies Library, Australian National University.

15. Discussions with older union activists in the late 1990s and early 2000s and with older PSI people frequently included references to different organizers who appeared to be in the same lineage.

16. The Indonesian party system, which had already banned left-wing parties in 1965, underwent another enforced simplification in the 1970s. Legislation was introduced allowing only three political parties.

17. Princen also established and ran a human rights monitoring and advocacy organization in the 1980s.

18. For a history of the PRD, see Lane, *Unfinished Nation*.

19. See the chapter "Aksi" in Lane, *Unfinished Nation*.

20. Budiman Sujatmiko was the national chairperson of the PRD during the New Order period. This was the main national spokesperson position for the PRD. After 1996, Indrakusuma and Warouw were both high on the police's official List of Sought After People (DPO— Daftar Pencarian Orang), but they were not found to be detained.

21. https://kasbi.or.id/.

22. http://sentralgerakanburuhnasional.blogspot.com.au/.

23. All of these unions have experienced splits and regroupments, often

connected to developments within the political organization to which they were connected. The URL of the FBLP's Facebook page is https://www.facebook.com/permalink.php?id=403380686341825&story_fbid=668191206527437.

24. Such as the time when the PRD-SMID-PPBI network gave critical support to Megawati Sukarnoputri during her period of resistance against Suharto, 1996–98.

25. There were, of course, some workers who had become involved in day-to-day union activity, with the small number of employers who took the industrial relations law seriously. Anecdotal reports from some workers indicate that most of these were larger workplaces, with higher levels of division of labour, usually owned by companies from the advanced industrialized nations. There is no available data from the 1980s and 1990s to make a quantitative assessment of this.

26. Johannes Nicolaas Warouw, *Assuming Modernity: Migrant Industrial Workers in Tangerang* (PhD dissertation, Australian National University, Indonesia, 2004). Warouw, who had been familiar with worker protest activity in the 1990s as a PRD activist, documented in his research after 2000 that a new generation of workers, at least in the factories he researched, was uninterested in militant or strike activity.

Chapter 2

Transition Out of State Authoritarian Unionism

The manner in which the New Order fell, the policy changes towards trade unions that occurred in 1998 under President Habibie, and the new economic situation impacted on the pre-existing labour politics to change their terrain fundamentally. Most obviously, the policy of having only a single union ended, allowing the formation of a range of unions independent of each other. However, the change was more significant than that. New processes were set in motion that, while unfolding slowly and with difficulty, are already dramatically transforming trade union politics, and potentially may change national politics in general.

The Fall of the New Order

The thirty-three years of authoritarianism under Suharto did not end as part of a planned succession. Suharto departed the scene accompanied by significant turmoil and rejection of the old authoritarian order. The slogan of the process that brought him down was: *Reformasi!* (Reformation), implying a deep reform to policy and methods of rule. Withdrawal of the armed forces from politics, in particular from political control (repression), and withdrawal of laws curtailing political freedoms were central demands of most protests, along with a demand to end corruption and cronyism. Between June 1996 and May 1998, hundreds of thousands of people participated in street mobilizations and other actions. While many were students, the vast majority were from the working class, employed, underemployed or unemployed.[1]

Suharto's being pushed into resignation after an extended period of oppositional mobilization involving large numbers of the working population meant that there remained a dynamic contributing to ongoing worker protests. Despite the fact that the existing large union, the FSPSI, was anti-mobilization, that the SBSI was cautious about it, and that the PPBI was small and more an organizing centre than a consolidated member-based organization, worker protests continued in the period immediately after the fall of Suharto. Such protests were carried out either by workers at single factories organizing independently or, in the majority of organized cases, by the PPBI. The press reported strikes and protests in most months from June through to December even in 1998. In fact, there was a significant increase in such activity compared to the previous year.[2]

The activity, which continued until around 2001, also manifested in the establishing of new unions, especially enterprise unions. This was facilitated by significant changes in the legal regime.

Repression Weakens during Habibie Interregnum and After

B.J. Habibie was president for eighteen months, from 21 May 1998 until 20 October 1999. He acceded to the presidency on the resignation of President Suharto. Habibie was vice-president at that time. Parliamentary elections were held in October 1999, and the People's Consultative Assembly (MPR) elected a new president, Abdurrahman Wahid. There were, as might be expected, two dynamics operating during these eighteen months regarding government policy towards labour.

The resignation of Suharto satisfied the immediate and major demand of the protest movement. This resulted in the rapid demobilization of the movement, with the expectation that other reforms would take place subsequently. An atmosphere of mobilization did continue, however, among its most militant elements. The protest movement did not reach the stage of an insurrection to seize power, even in terms of the structures of governance, let alone social and economic structures. Suharto's resignation saved the existing structures, except, eventually, for the privileged position previously enjoyed by the armed forces and the government party, GOLKAR—and the official union leaderships. While the armed forces eventually lost their privileged position in the political structure, in the period 1998–2001 they were still in a position to continue many New Order policies. The same applied to the civilian state apparatus; for example, the ministries.

In the interregnum, there were two dynamics regarding labour: unrevolutionized structures continuing the policies of the New Order and a new, contradictory, dynamic introduced by several dramatic policy decisions of President Habibie.

The continuity of old structures operated in both the arena of legislative activity and of repression. The central legislative issue was a proposed industrial relations law, Manpower Law No. 25/1997, formulated under Suharto. This was to replace the conglomeration of laws inherited from the pre-1965 period, which had only been amended or changed in practice by regulation—or ignored. Many of the pre-1965 laws favoured workers and were used by human rights activists in their criticisms of the New Order government. While trying to appear to conform to international standards, the regime aimed at ensuring tight control of labour. It was widely critiqued by human rights activists throughout 1997 and into 1998.[3] The new law was seen as a step towards codification of the relations between the regime, capital and labour that had evolved under authoritarian state unionism. The law had been passed by the time Habibie replaced Suharto, but it had not been enacted. There was a review under Habibie, but the decision was to enact the law, although its starting date was delayed from October 1998 until October 2000. The personnel of the Ministry of Manpower remained the same as under Suharto, as did the leadership of the armed forces and the composition of the parliament. This continuity should not be surprising. However, the delay must be seen as highly beneficial to a change in the labour scene, as during 1998 and 1999, Habibie made other decisions in this area.

The arena of institutional change had been the presidency, where both the president and his team of advisors changed. It was from this quarter that dramatic new changes were initiated— dramatic, given the legacy the New Order had left. The Habibie government ratified International Labour Organization (ILO) Convention 87 on the Freedom of Association and Protection of the Right to Organize. Rather than attempt to take this ratification through what was still a New Order era parliament, Habibie legalized the ratification in a formal presidential decision (Keppres No. 83/1998), implemented through a ministerial regulation (PER-05/MEN/1998). Other democratizing steps included announcing early elections (although communism was still banned, as were parties that lacked a national spread) and preparations for serious decentralization of government powers to lower levels. The package confirmed that there would be a serious liberalization of formal political arrangements.

Ratification of Convention 87 and delay of the 1997 Manpower Law facilitated a radical change in the union situation. However, pressures for continuity were still there, beginning to change seriously—and even then only partially—only after the 1999 elections. For example, the Manpower Ministry still had to approve the registration of new unions. Ford writes:

> The implications of the department's continued role in deciding which unions could register were immediately clear. While some informants had successfully registered and run small, independent unions following the Convention's ratification, others reported cases where registration had been rejected and the worker-activists involved dismissed The risks surrounding registration were high: workers wishing to register a union had to provide a list of its members' names as a condition of their application to register (Article 3 of PER-05/MEN/1998). Another notable feature of departmental policy during the Habibie interregnum was its continued refusal to permit alternative unions to register in workplaces where an SPSI unit existed. Informants reported that department officials had argued that the legality of more than one union in a workplace was still unclear although departmental responses varied from city to city.[4]

In fact, physical harassment by the military also continued, especially of strikes and protests. Manpower Ministry statistics indicate that strike numbers increased in 1998, probably partly reflecting the politicized atmosphere, before declining during the next few years (when a new, less politicized, workforce from rural areas was being absorbed and when the last wave of mobilizations stopped after the removal of President Wahid).

There were several examples of physical harassment and attacks on mobilizing workers. The ones that attracted the most protest were the interventions of armed soldiers against workers in two significant mobilizations in June 1998, just one month after Habibie's coming to power, when New Order momentum was still in effect and reacting to the mass protests that forced Suharto to resign.

The first action to be attacked was organized by KOBAR (Workers' Committee for Reformation Action), a coalition of activist worker groups. KOBAR included PPBI activists and forces, but also other worker groups. As its name signified, it came out of and identified with the *aksi massa* mobilizations against Suharto and for *Reformasi*. It organized a mass meeting in support of a series of demands. These were:

1. Increase the minimum wage by 100 per cent, to 11,500 rupiah per day.
2. Lower prices.
3. Stop sackings, and pay workers forced on leave.
4. End collusion between the Ministry of Manpower and employers.
5. End discrimination and oppression of women.
6. Repeal anti-worker labour laws.
7. Freedom of organization.
8. Free Dita Sari and other political prisoners.
9. End military intervention in worker disputes.
10. Open company books to workers.[5]

Working together with students from the University of Indonesia, KOBAR organized a mass meeting of workers to be held at the university campus on Jalan Salemba in central Jakarta. KOBAR's announcement stated that at least twelve thousand workers would attend from North Jakarta, Tangerang, East Jakarta, Bogor and Bekasi-Kerawang. The largest contingents were from North Jakarta and Tangerang. The meeting was blocked by a large mobilization of armed troops. KOBAR reported that in some areas where buses were waiting to pick up workers, they were physically attacked, with both workers and students being injured. Most workers were unable to depart, and only a few hundred made it to the university. Armed soldiers blocked the entrances to the campus.

Three days later, the same fate befell a mass meeting being organized by the SBSI. This also was for demands around corruption and labour laws, and called for President Habibie to form a government based on a Council of National Reconciliation—a more political demand than SBSI normally advocated. Its secretariat was surrounded by armed soldiers, and the street to its office was blocked off; workers who had arrived by bus were prevented from reaching the office.

While this reflected continuity with New Order practices, the ability of KOBAR and SBSI to denounce these actions publicly without repressive consequences reflected the new democratic space. Repression and conflict had not ended, but the space in which conflict could unfold had been expanded. Additionally, while harassment and military intervention continued, they did steadily decline, despite the fact that the KOBAR and SBSI actions in June and others by students and workers in the coming months were part of a revived wave of mobilizations that led to massive marches in November that occupied the parliamentary buildings. These were demobilized only when it became clear that Habibie and the mainstream opposition figures had settled on a definite process towards elections.

Such contradictory policies were primarily a consequence of the transitional nature of the period and the relative isolation of a reformist presidency. There is little doubt, though, that the decision to ratify ILO Convention 87 was the key development, overshadowing the resistance to change from within the bureaucracy, the armed forces and business. Neither then nor till today have physical harassment and even attempts to jail protesting workers stopped. Nor are many labour policies friendly towards workers, including on key issues such as the minimum wage and illegal labour hire. Indonesian governments are not social democratic, with links to a strong union movement (which does not exist), let alone socialist. Labour policy is formulated in response to direct pressures from domestic social or international forces. Ironically, perhaps the exception to this was Habibie's ratification of Convention 87, which does not seem to have been necessary to placate serious pressure from below or from outside Indonesia.

The ratification did mean, however, *the end to the most central aspects of the New Order trade union system*. It ended state support for a particular union and its leadership. It ended a system which de facto allowed only one union. Regulations creating obstacles for unions were there, as they are even in countries with strong union traditions. However, the ratification rent asunder the old system. The most obvious manifestation of this was the reorganization, from within the FSPSI and at the factory level, of the trade union terrain.

A New Union Terrain

There is still a great deal not fully known about the emergence of new and reformed unions. In a country as large as Indonesia and with tens of thousands of workplaces, many unions are registered purely as single enterprise unions or regional union federations. There may also be large numbers of smaller unions not registered or in the process of registration even today. Precisely what activity they carry out week to week is undocumented. Information on union activities is mainly available around the activities of the major confederations and their constituent federations, and some more active federations that are not affiliated to a confederation.

Enterprise unions register independently. They can come together in a federation, mostly along (rather loose) sectoral lines. Federations can then come together to form confederations. However, there is no legal obligation for enterprise unions to federate. Also, while the bureaucratic processes are complex and operate as a disincentive to disaffiliating from a federation, it is possible to do so. Also, more than one union can organize and be registered in a workplace.

While the introductory map of the current union terrain and some of its origins focuses on the major confederations and federations, it is extremely important to note the existence of a large number of non-federated or locally federated unions. This phenomenon is a crucial part of the current terrain, even if at any one time major initiatives in changing the situation come from the confederations and federations. The reason for emphasizing this is to draw attention to a key feature of the current situation that is also related to the legacies of the New Order discussed in the previous chapter. The mushrooming of unions is a direct consequence of the enforced artificiality of the structure that existed under the New Order. The state-protected single union never covered all workplaces, and even where it did have coverage, its presence was mostly "artificially" imposed and consequently fragile. Once state protection disappeared, this fragility was revealed. When, in 2000, new legislation allowed a union to register with just ten members, this new situation was further facilitated and legitimized.

Within several years of that legislation, there were at least ninety registered union federations and four registered confederations. By 2017 there were fourteen confederations. There are undoubtedly even more enterprise unions. While the union with the largest dues-paying membership is still the main bloc coming out of the pre-1998 FSPI, namely the KSPSI, there is certainly no longer an enforced single union monopoly.

Despite some continuity, *the union movement is to all intents and purposes renewing.* This new terrain has been formed out of at least three processes.

One process has been the regroupment of the FSPSI constituency, supplemented by the integration of some of the newly formed enterprise unions. Data is not available on the balance in the federations originating from the FSPSI between union members of workplaces previously and newly affiliated to the FSPSI. In some ways, this data may also no longer be key, because there have also been important sociological changes in the composition of the workforce since the Asian financial crisis (*krismon*) in 1997. The continuity between FSPSI and today's FSPI-originating unions may relate more to key aspects of the legacy, such as the lack of tradition of leader-membership accountability and an orientation to protection from above, rather than a continuity of factory personnel. What continuity of personnel does exist has been frayed, fragmented and diluted as a result of the mass dismissals of 1997–98 and then new waves of recruitment after 2000.

A second process has been regroupment as well as polarization among unions whose origins can be traced back to the dissident trends before 1998. The continuity is via both personnel and ideology, especially because many of the individuals who have played leadership roles have always been ideologically oriented. At least two confederations today, KASBI and KPBI, have their origins in this process. There are also federations and individuals who differentiate ideologically, and in some cases are a product of polarizations and splits within what might be called a left union current (see Table 2.1.)

The third process, which I am not able to discuss, is the fragmentation that sustains a large number of smaller or enterprise-based unions and federations. Sometimes these are identifiable by their ideological orientation, such as Islamic, or connected to pre-1965 ideologies, such as Marhaenism. Some appear simply as sectoral federations or enterprise unions. In both cases, their internal ideological composition and week-to-week activities are beyond the scope of this essay. A very large research team would be needed to collect the data, and in any case, given that everything is still so new, their situation can also change very rapidly.

Reorganization of the State-Protected Union Constituency

Ford provides a useful inventory of the new unions that emerged out of this constituency after 1998.[6] Even by September 1998, eleven federations had registered under the new regulations. By February 1999, the number had increased to fifteen and by March to seventeen. As indicated above, by 2015, ninety were registered. The FSPSI itself had split by August 1998, creating the FSPSI-Reformasi.[7] So within just a few months of Suharto's fall, the fragility of the structure, once the state abandoned a direct role, was quickly exhibited. Another example of the fragility was the break-up of the Korps Pegawai Negeri Indonesia (KORPRI— Indonesian Civil Service Corps). This was an association of all members of the civil service, who had been obliged to join under the New Order. It did not pretend to be a union, but rather was integrated into the state political party, GOLKAR, as a part of a system of political support for the government. After May 1998, however, its fragility was also exposed. Employees in some state-owned enterprises broke away and formed unions. Ford lists some of these to include Garuda Airlines employees and port and maritime workers. In June 1999, a Federasi Serikat Pekerja–Badan Usaha Milik Negara (FSP-BUMN—Federation of State-Owned Enterprise Trade Unions) was formed. In just over a year after the fall of Suharto, even in the directly owned state sector, the state-protected organization of employees was crumbling.

An additional new development was the rapid emergence of white-collar unions, covering the banking and finance sectors, which were particularly active in the first years after Suharto's fall.

Between 1999 and today, both the FSPSI and the FSPSI-Reformasi went through further changes. Their two key manifestations after 2010 have been the Konfederasi Serikat Perkera Seluruh Indonesia (KSPSI—All-Indonesia Trade Union Confederation) and the Konfederasi Serikat Perkerja Indonesia (KSPI—Confederation of Indonesian Trade Unions), coming via the SPSI-Reformasi. The route from SPSI-Reformasi to KSPI was very messy. The SPSI-Reformasi eventually started to disintegrate. Some of the sectoral federations split one by one. Out of some of these splits, the KSPI was eventually formed, driven by the FSPMI, which was headed by a former SPSI central official, Tharmin Mosi. The current president, Said Iqbal, was secretary-general.[8] The precise phases and twists and turns between 1999 and today are beyond the scope of this essay. For understanding the basic dynamics, the crucial point is that the old FSPSI has re-formed, under new leaders and new conditions, into two blocs. Basic features and key aspects of the political activities of these two blocs will be discussed below. One key factor is that the FSPSI-Reformasi federations in the manufacturing sector quickly secured coverage over the largest manufacturing (i.e., assembly) plants with the best potential bargaining position, such as the automobile and motor bike assembly plants. Most activist observers assess that the KSPSI has the largest membership. The KSPI has won the biggest campaigning profile, especially since 2011–12.

It is very likely that some workplaces covered by the pre-1998 FSPSI may no longer be covered by either KSPSI or KSPI, but by other of the smaller federations. And, of course, there are new workplaces that have formed, especially after the few years of downturn following the 1997 *krismon*.[9]

The two confederations' overall political frameworks are, however, similar; namely, working for incremental improvements within the existing political economy. In relation to the immediate political format that emerged after the New Order, their histories have been different. The KSPSI's leadership has maintained contacts either with GOLKAR or with the PDIP. Elite internal conflicts have sometimes reflected a tension between leaders with these different affiliations. The KSPI, whose political evolution will be discussed in more depth below, had a more pragmatic evolution. Individual leaders have had separate political party ties; for example, its current president having stood as a candidate for the Islamic Justice Party in national elections in 2009.[10] However, as an organization it has passed through different phases. From the 2000s until 2011–12, it frequently allied with the maverick PDIP member of parliament Rieke Pithaloka, and also with social democratic-oriented NGOs. In 2013 it swung into an alliance with Prabowo Subianto, the leader of GERINDRA, which was also in coalition with the PKS. In the 2014 presidential elections, it supported Prabowo Subianto. In the 2014 parliamentary elections, it negotiated for five of its members to stand as candidates for several different parties.[11]

It can be argued that by 2017 both the KSPI and the KSPSI had settled on an orientation to one or another of the factions of the political ruling class, as organized through parties. While one of their officials, Obon Tabrani, stood as an independent candidate in the 2017 local elections,[12] this does not appear to have altered the institutional alliance with Prabowo's GERINDRA.

Reorganization of Dissident Unionism after 1998

It is necessary to grasp the emergence of trade unions as a whole since the 1990s as essentially a political phenomenon, the development of which goes back to the repression of mass organizing that took place immediately after 1965. Equally, prior to 1998, the emergence of dissident trade unionism was intimately connected with the rise of opposition to New Order authoritarianism. One way to see this process is that "nascent organizing" helped politicize labour issues.[13] However, this approach separates the dissident union organizing from the deeper political processes relating to democratization. Dissident unionism in the Suharto years can be divided into two streams by their different approaches to authoritarianism. The SBSI's orientation was a focus on improvement of wages and conditions, which required more democracy. The PPBI's approach was that radical structural change was needed in order for workers, and the whole population, to be able to start to solve their social and economic problems. This also needed greater democratic space, not simply so that wages and conditions could be improved but so that ideological and political struggle could seek to win structural change. In this second framework, the organization and mobilization of workers (the vast majority of the population in one form or another) was a force that could bring about that change. The PPBI acted more as a struggle centre than a traditional trade union. This differentiation was reflected in the post-1998 history of the SBSI and the PPBI. In the PPBI's case, that tradition has evolved multiple manifestations, with several new entities, sometimes emerging out of splits, and always reflecting differing ideological-cum-tactical orientations to overall political change.

Serikat Buruh Sejahtera Indonesia (SBSI)

The SBSI was formed in 1992 out of a coalition of non-government organizations, worker organizers and human rights activists. Its first president was Dr Muchtar Pakpahan, a lawyer and former activist in the Protestant Student Movement Organization operating in the New Order period. Pakpahan was jailed under Suharto and released under Habibie. The SBSI continued at one level or another throughout this period. At the time that Habibie signed Convention 87, the SBSI itself claimed 300,000 members organized in eleven federations. By that time also, it had federated to the International Federation of Christian Trade Unions and had links with the Dutch Christian trade union.

The SBSI was a part of the spectrum of groups pressing the Habibie government for democratic reform in 1998–99. As the political situation stabilized, SBSI also set about stabilizing itself as a trade union concentrating on improving wages and conditions at the site of production and lobbying for improvements in welfare policies. While involved in some major strikes in the late 1990s, organizing major national strike activity has not been a feature of its efforts since the mid-2000s.[14] The SBSI also experienced a split in 2003, in which a breakaway group established the SBSI 1992.[15] SBSI remains the more high-profile organization. As of 2019, it is difficult to assess which of SBSI and SBSI 1992 has the largest membership or is the most active.

In 2019 the SBSI's industrial strategy is not dissimilar to that of the FSPSI descended unions, the KSPSI and KPSI. It concentrates on workplace issues and national welfare policy.

Its overall framework is therefore similar; namely, working for incremental improvements within the existing political economy. However, its political orientation within the post–New Order political framework has evolved very differently from those of either the KSPI or the KSPSI. While the last two have settled on orientations to parts of the elite political coalitions, the SBSI has maintained a more independent position. This is not to say that the SBSI has not taken positions regarding national and local electoral contests—for example, the SBSI supported Joko Widodo as a presidential candidate—but it has also striven, within its resources and outlook, to build an independent base. From 1999, for example, its leadership, including Pakpahan, formed a labour party, which stood candidates in elections and is still a registered party. In 2016–17 it was in negotiation with other smaller political groups to bolster this formation. These other groups include the PRP and the Sarekat Hijau.

In this sense, the SBSI can be said still to work in an orthodox social democratic framework: campaigning for wages and conditions at the workplace through the union, and for welfare policy through both the union and a parliamentary labour party. To date, however, their Partai Buruh (Workers' Party) has not won any seats in the national parliament.

Dissident Unions and Radical Politics

The trade unions that emerged out of more radical political opposition to the New Order, and retaining a more left-wing criticism of capitalism, were a minority current before 1998, although their ability to identify demands, slogans and tactics that struck a chord with a large section of the working masses made them a vanguard during 1992–98 in the context of the deepening popular hostility to the New Order's political and socio-economic policies. Once the New Order was defeated and a new political format began to emerge, there was no longer the same scope for leadership by a small militant group.

The PPBI, as part of the PRD-PPBI-SMID network, dominated this tendency in 1998. It played a major role in the early 1998–99 worker coalitions, such as KOBAR. In the post–New Order period, however, pressures developed for the formulation of a new orientation to the general political framework. Between May 1998 and November 1998, the focus was on organizing another wave of mobilizations for the November special session of the MPR, with the aim of forcing the elite opposition forces (represented by Abdurrahman Wahid, Megawati Sukarnoputri and Amien Rais) to take power from Habibie and form a new government that would break continuity with the New Order structures. Those mobilizations did take place in November, and on a very large scale, but the three elite opposition figures distanced themselves from this effort, and the movement for an emergency government collapsed. The transition out of dictatorship would be via elections organized by the Habibie government. That decision by the combined elite groups stabilized the situation.

Once that stability was confirmed, which it was once an election law was passed, pressures to reformulate a radical political line increased within the PRD. Additionally, the intense politicization of the previous eighteen months or more had produced other centres of radical or left activism. Within a few years, while the PRD was the highest-profile group on the left, others had emerged, such as the grouping now known as the Pusat Perjuangan Indonesia (PPI—Indonesian Struggle Centre), some of whose founders came out of the anti-Suharto campus coalitions of 1998.

The PRD, like Pakpahan's Partai Buruh, stood in the 1999 elections. However, neither party made any headway, and they were swamped by the spectrum of parties with financial resources or access to the masses through traditional or pre-existing social networks and groups. In the wake of this pressure, there were more debates and discussions about what to do next. This eventually resulted in a series of splits and resignations from the PRD. Over fifteen years, new groups formed by splits would also recruit from new generations of activists, including recruiting leaders. These developments are important for understanding the current map of trade unions, as many of these groups either took their worker base with them or started anew in building unions.

The splits and regroupments went through various phases, provoked by a range of issues. As of 2019, we can identify the political groups that have important historical links, in one way or another, with the PRD-PPBI-SMID network, and that have played a role in the development of the more radical union stream.

The Partai Rakyat Pekerja, which was formed in 2004 by ex-leaders of the PRD alongside activists from a new generation, played an important role in the establishment and development of KASBI. In 2011 the PRP split and a new group was formed, the KPO-PRP.[16] Both are still active today. KASBI aligned initially with the KPO-PRP, which, they argued, advocated more of a mass campaigning orientation than the PRP. Central organizers from the old PPBI and former PRD members played important roles during the emergence of KASBI. Later, KASBI broke away from KPO-PRP to operate unaligned with any political bloc. One long-term PPBI organizer stayed with KASBI, another with KPO-PRP. By 2017, however, and indeed since earlier, KASBI had recruited many new people and formed a leadership group in which ex-PPBI/PRD people operated primarily as individuals. In the meantime, both the PRP and the KPO-PRP continued to organize enterprise unions and form their own federations.[17]

Thus, as a result of the formation of the PRP as a "rival" to the PRD on the left, three new union formations emerged. KASBI is easily the biggest of these. It is able to mobilize relatively large numbers at rallies and demonstrations and its job-site activism is no less than others.

The PPBI itself, formally connected to the PRD, reorganized as the FNPBI. Its chairperson was PRD and labour movement spokesperson and former political prisoner Dita Sari. The FNPBI started building a more traditional trade union structure, especially after 1999. It came under some pressure initially from the United States' AFL-CIO to distance itself from the PRD, but this pressure did not succeed. At the same time, the new difficulties of organizing a radical left party in the stabilized *Reformasi* period led to some resignations, as key PRD figures either shifted to non-government work, entered the media or universities or shifted to one of the elite parties. The party went through an early split leading to the failed attempt to form the Democratic Socialist Party (PDS), some of whose key figures later became involved in the PRP.

The PRD suffered its most serious split in 2007, when a significant number of members and leaders were expelled when they opposed a policy to reorient the party and stand members in elections via another party that carried a conservative, Islamic banner.[18] This resulted in a major weakening of the party. After the failure of this electoral tactic to gain any seats for PRD members in 2008, Dita Sari, who had been strongly identified with the FNPBI, left the PRD and campaigned for GOLKAR.[19]

This evolution of the PRD between 2000 and 2010 made its trade union work almost impossible. By 2019 it would be difficult to identify any significant union activity associated with the PRD as it is today, a more nationalist than left radical group.[20]

The members expelled from the PRD reorganized as a new grouping and continued to organize a union base. Although they too experienced a split in 2012, the union organizing has continued. One wing of the split, known as Politik Rakyat (People's Politics), has continued union organizing, especially in factories with a large female workforce. Their members lead formal union and worker organizations, in the Federasi Buruh Lintas Pabrik (FBLP—Cross-Factory Workers' Federation). They also manage a community radio station aimed at factory workers.

The other component from the 2012 split, uniting with some who had earlier resigned from the political organization, also continued union work. In 2019 this group is the Partai Pembebasan Rakyat (PPR—People's Liberation Party). The evolution of their union work has been more complicated. Initially this group included a small union formation, covering mainly food processing workers. It also included individuals who worked in the automobile sector. In addition, one central leader, Danial Indrakusuma, who left the grouping before the 2012 split, had become active in the educational activities, and some organizing, in the Federasi Serikat Pekerja Metal Indonesia (FSPMI—Indonesian Metal Workers' Union Federation), which was the largest and best organized union in the KSPI. Starting in around 2010, he played an increasingly important role in some of the union's activities. He was initiated into the Garda Metal, a uniformed spearhead group for the FSPMI, which led all street demonstrations. Thousands of workers attended "Ekopol"[21] courses taught by Indrakusuma.[22] During 2010–17, they had no connection with any political bloc, having left the group that formed a few years after the 2007 expulsions. But in 2018 they joined the PPR. This meant that the PPR had two involvements, through the small union its members directly led and through the activities of its new recruits in the FSPMI. This ended in 2014 when Indrakusma and a co-worker, along with several other external collaborators with the FSPMI, were "excommunicated".[23] The association with the FSPMI increased the networking of the PPR activists in this arena, so that from 2016 they were able to establish a new union of their own. However, this was not the primary aim of the association with the FSPMI, which was rather to equip the latter with the methods of struggle and ideas that the PPBI-PRD-SMID leadership core had developed before 1998.

As we will see in the next chapter, although involving very few people, the association between the former PRD-PPBI activists and the FSPMI was very important. It was probably the key example of cross-fertilization between the stream of union activity coming out of the reconstitution and further evolution of the SPSI constituency and the radical wing of the dissident union stream, which had emphasized resistance (*perlawanan*) to the New Order. This was not the only cross-fertilization between the SPSI descendants' stream and the thinking that traced its origins to the anti–New Order movement. There was also an association between the FSPMI and the Trade Union Rights Centre (TURC), staffed by activists who had earlier been in the Lembaga Bantuan Hukum (LBH—Legal Aid Institute) in Jakarta, an NGO that had always been open to the more radical elements. And while TURC activists were not of the same ideological outlook as the PRD-PPBI activists, they could still trace their origins to that pre-1998 resistance milieu.[24] This association, and the consequent ideological impact on the FSPMI, later ended with a break between the FSPMI and individuals with backgrounds from the PRD-PPBI and the TURC, and others. The FSPMI leadership even issued an instruction that no FSPMI member was to have anything to do with these people without permission. No reasons were given. The context of this break will be discussed below. At this point we can note that this current coming out of the PRD-PPBI has a role in leading two unions, SEDAR and Gabungan Solidaritas Perjuangan Buruh (GSPB—Workers' Struggle Solidarity Association).[25] Among the leadership are members of the PPR, former members of the PPR and "graduates" of PPR-influenced education courses, as well as unaligned workers.

Another of the unions originating from this stream is the Serikat Buruh Transportasi Perjuangan Indonesia (SBTPI— Indonesian Struggle Transport Workers Union). The core of this union's membership is made up of truck and crane drivers servicing Jakarta's main port, as well as crane and other warehouse vehicle drivers in and around the ports. At its founding congress in 2005, Ilham Syah was elected its president. He too was a member of the PRD in the 1990s. The influence of the radical stream of the 1990s was reflected in the first of three slogans the SBTPI adopted at the congress: "Melawan Penjajahan Baru (Neo-liberalisme)" (Oppose the New Occupation—Neo-Liberalism). The SBTPI remains an important union, playing a role in the formation of a port workers' union federation, which includes four other port worker unions. Politically more significant was its role in the establishment in 2016 of the KPBI. This new confederation brought together several of the unions connected to groups that emerged out of the radical opposition to the New Order. Members of the KPBI include the SBTPI/FBPI and the FLBP, among others, but not SEDAR.

The Federasi Perjuangan Buruh Indonesia (FPBI—Indonesian Workers' Struggle Federation) is one of two unions with a more radical politics that has no connection with the 1990s PRD-PPBI network. It is aligned with the PPI, formed by activists who played a role in a cross-campus student alliance in 1998, in particular the Forum Kota. There is also an active nationwide student formation aligned with the PPI.

A further federation that came out of the radical opposition in the 1990s to the New Order is the Gabungan Serikat Buruh Indonesia (GSBI—Indonesian Association of Trade Unions), first formed as the Gabungan Serikat Buruh Independen in March 1999. It was connected to a current of activism that had placed ideological emphasis on the peasantry as an agency of change and had been active in peasant activism, but it has also organized among workers.

The unions that have come out of this dissident current are set out in Table 2.1.

TABLE 2.1
Unions with Origins Connected to the Anti–New Order Radicalism of the 1990s

Union	Connection
SGBN/Progresip	KPO-PRP (Jabatabek)
KSN	PRP
Sedar	PPR
GSBN	PPI
KASBI	Originally PRP, then KPO-PRP, now unaligned
FBLP	Politik Rakyat
SBTPI–FBTI	Unaligned
GSBI	Front Perjuangan Rakyat
FNPBI	PRD

TABLE 2.2
Politically Significant Confederations as of 2019

Konfederasi Serikat Pekerja Seluruh Indonesia (KSPSI)
Konfederasi Serikat Pekerja Indonesia (KSPI)
Konfederasi Persatuan Buruh Indonesia (KPBI)
Konfederasi Buruh Sejahtera Indonesia (KSBSI)
Konfederasi Serikat Nasional (KSN—National Union Federation).

Remembering the Sociological Legacy:
Krismon and After

There are many more regional, local and factory unions than I have discussed above. There have also been many temporary alliances of unions, large and small, during the period up to 2017. The number and diversity of unions make a sharp contrast with the basically single, state-backed union situation that existed before 1998. The map sketched out in this essay is oriented to describing what exists today, but it will already be clear that the pre-1998 terrain was recast very quickly, starting within months of the fall of Suharto. This number and diversity of unions and their groupings, despite some continuity, underline the newness and fluidity of this terrain.

Another factor adding to the newness and fluidity is the sociological changes impacting on the working class, brought about by the economic developments during this period. Huge numbers of new workers have entered the workforce. Following the Asian economic crisis, there was a significant drop in the factory workforce. At the time, the district of Tangerang was where manufacturing was centred. According to the Tangerang Statistics Bureau, the manufacturing workforce in 1995 and 1996 was around 202,000. Over the three years after the 1997 economic crisis, the workforce dropped to 170,000.[26] As manufacturing slowly started to pick up from 2000 onwards, a new generation of workers was drawn from the small towns and villages of Java, southern Sumatra and southern Sulawesi. As Warouw has vividly portrayed in his work on Tangerang factory workers in 2002, these workers brought with them a village and small town consciousness. Warouw paints a very complex picture of change in social and cultural consciousness in the tug-of-war process along the rural and urban continuum. Among the workers he observed over an extended period in the early 2000s, organized militancy was not the norm. Rather, the social readjustment from rural or small town to a new urbanized setting defined their reality. Most were also still young. A significant proportion had senior high school education in their home town, others having only junior high school or primary schooling. A tiny percentage had university or vocational college training. Statistics and newspaper reports indicate that strikes were taking place in this period, but it is also clear that the sociological recomposition of the workforce in the Tangerang area, then expanding to neighbouring Karawang, was at least an equally dominant aspect of reality, and, indeed, perhaps the most dominant aspect for workers at that time.

Warouw's thorough research makes little mention of experience or memory among the Tangerang workers of the anti–New Order political mobilizations of the 1990s, which were concentrated in the larger cities. Thus, we can add another component of the diversity among the workforce in the Jakarta factory-belt areas. There are workers with experience of the 1990s mobilizations and those who have no such experience. Given the expansion of the factory workforce since 2000, it must be concluded that the overwhelming majority can be classified as "new", entering the factory after the fall of Suharto and in a period of expansion of manufacturing, compared to the 1990s, even though while remaining very small in the total workforce.

In 2000, the manufacturing workforce in Tangerang municipality was 170,000. In 2015 it was measured as being 317,000. Manufacture is now spread throughout several areas of Tangerang district, outside the town also, and official statistics give a figure of 673,584 employed in manufacturing.[27] Manufacture has also spread to Karawang district, where 242,896 are noted as employed in manufacturing.[28] Between 2003 and 2014, the number of medium and large enterprises increased from 228 to 542.[29] Employment in medium to small enterprises in Karawang grew from 87,427 in 2003 to 203,889 in 2014.[30] There may be a million more workers who have gathered in Tangerang and Karawang over the last ten to fifteen years, not counting workers in other factory-intense areas, such as North Jakarta. By definition, all these workers will be inexperienced in most aspects of life in a factory belt near a big city and, crucially, have no experience of unionism. Neither would their parents or grandparents have had any experience of unionism.

This sociological aspect, the composition of the workforce, adds another dimension to the newness that characterizes the terrain of union and labour politics in Indonesia.

Notes

1. The absence from these protests of workers organized through trade unions has led some analysts to conclude that workers, or the working class, played no role in the downfall of Suharto. See Edward Aspinall, "Democratisation, the Working Class and the Indonesian Crisis", *Review of Indonesian and Malaysian Affairs* 33, no. 2 (1999): 1–32; also, Olle Tôrnquist, "Workers in Politics: Why is Organised Labour Missing from the Democratic Movement?", *Inside Indonesia* 86 (April–June 2006). This approach assumes that the only way that workers can assert their political presence is through trade unions. For an analysis of the role of workers in the dislodging of Suharto, see Max Lane, "Indonesia and the Fall of Suharto: Proletarian Politics in the 'Planet of Slums' Era", *Journal of Labour and Society* 13, no. 2 (June 2010): 185–200.

2. See, for example, such English language reports as in *Tapol*, 24 June 1998; *Dow Jones Newswires*, 4 June 1998; *Jakarta Post*, 12 October 1998. For statistics on strike activity, see Johannes Nicolaas Warouw, "Assuming Modernity: Migrant Industrial Workers in Tangerang,

Indonesia" (PhD dissertation, Australian National University, 2004), http://hdl.handle.net/1885/9954, p. 27.

3. Michele Ford, *Workers and Intellectuals: NGOs, Trade Unions and the Indonesian Labour Movement* (Singapore: NUS Press/Hawai'i University Press/KITLV, 2009), pp. 66–67.

4. Ibid., p. 73.

5. KOMITE BURUH untuk AKSI REFORMASI (KOBAR) No: 04/ KOBAR/I/1998 Hal: Pernyataan Sikap dan Klarifikasi [Statement of position and clarification], available at https://www.library.ohio.edu/ indopubs/1998/06/25/0031.html.

6. Ford, *Workers and Intellectuals*, p. 200.

7. "Sectoral Unions Break from FSPSI", *Jakarta Post*, 22 August 1998.

8. There was probably a FSPMI strategy of splitting the sectoral unions of the SPSI at the base, in key areas such as automobile assembly. At least one plant, Yamaha, still has both the KSPSI and KSPI unions registered and with members in that plant. Information from interview with informant, Bekasi.

9. See Warouw, "Assuming Modernity" for pre-2002 data.

10. See Ford, *Workers and Intellectuals*.

11. These developments are covered in more detail below.

12. Amalinda Savarini, "Melawan Oligarki dan Pragmatisme Warga: Gerakan Buruh di Pilkada Kabupaten Bekasi 2017", *Indoprogress*, May 2017, https://indoprogress.com/2017/05/melawan-oligarki-dan-pragmatisme-warga-gerakan-buruh-di-pilkada-kabupaten-bekasi-2017/.

13. Michele Ford, "Economic Unionism and Labour's Poor Performance in Indonesia's 1999 and 2004 Elections", http://airaanz.econ.usyd.edu.au/papers/Ford.pdf. This is an early paper that implicitly defines "political unions" within a framework of electoralism.

14. Strike activity from workplace to workplace is not publicly documented, so this impression is based on media reporting and union activist perceptions.

15. http://arishadiono.blogspot.co.id/2014/05/profil-sbsi-1992_3.html.

16. Some factories stayed with the PRP. The confederation affiliated to the PRP today is the Konfederasi Serikat Nasional (KSN—National Union Confederation).

17. The PRP leads the KSN, and the KPO-PRP leads Federasi Progresip and SGBN.

18. Max Lane, *Unfinished Nation: Ingatan Revolusi, Aksi Massa dan Sejarah Indonesia* (Djaman Baroe, 2014).

19. Ibid.

20. The most visible manifestation of the post-2007 PRD, under the leadership of Jabo, is *Berdirikari Online*, its web magazine. The magazine publishes articles that could be described as "left nationalist". There is very little media coverage of the PRD's activities.

21. "Ekopol" was an educational curriculum that had evolved out of the PRD's and Indrakusuma's political work since the 1990s. It covered economic theory and political history.

22. Indrakusuma was later joined by another former activist in the pre-split group, Sarinah, now coordinator of the worker news website, solidaritas.net (2015–17).

23. For the official excommunication instruction, see "Email from Said Iqbal to FSPMI Branches No.:01835/Org/DPP FSPMI/VIII/2014Hal: Instruksi organisasi", reproduced in David Duncan, "Out of the Factory, Onto the Streets: The Indonesian Metalworkers Union Federation (FSPMI) as a Case of Union Revitalisation in Indonesia" (BA Hons. thesis, 2015), p. 87.

24. The connection with this milieu was reflected in LBH lawyer activist and later TURC director, Surya Candra, being present in 2001 at an international seminar on Asia Pacific political developments in Sawangan outside Jakarta organized by PRD activists. Candra acted for detained international participants after the seminar was raided by police, immigration and Islamic militia. In 2014 the TURC was active propagating the Workers Party of Brazil as a model for Indonesia.

25. As of 2017/2018, the leadership connection between GSPB and the PPR milieu no longer exists.

26. https://tangerangkota.bps.go.id/linkTableDinamis/view/id/22.
27. Ibid.
28. https://tangerangkab.bps.go.id/linkTabelStatis/view/id/21.
29. https://karawangkab.bps.go.id/linkTabelStatis/view/id/76.
30. https://karawangkab.bps.go.id/linkTabelStatis/view/id/266.

Chapter 3

The Rise and Decline of Union Militancy, 2010–13

From Consolidation to Campaigning

The years 1998–2010 were a period of reorganization, re-composition and consolidation for the larger confederations. The unions that evolved from the dissident unionism and radical oppositional politics of the 1990s had a more fluid experience. There is less clear data available regarding the other, less political, confederations, federations and unaffiliated unions. For the larger confederations, especially the KSPSI and KSPI, and also for KSBSI, recomposition and consolidation had more or less been completed by 2010. Their structures, leaderships, international affiliations and mechanisms for collecting dues had settled. Their week-to-week work at the factory site, training and public advocacy were all ongoing—constrained primarily by their emphasis on consolidation following the 1998 end of the old system.[1]

By 2010 a new post-consolidation situation arose. How were they to take their development further? The first campaigning issue for the new consolidated unions was the Bill on Social Security Providers (BPJS Bill). This was to establish the provider mechanisms following the passing of Law No. 40/2004 on a National Social Security System (SJSN Law).[2] The SJSN Law required that all Indonesians be covered by social security through five mandatory universal programmes: healthcare benefits, occupational accident benefits, old age risk benefits, pension benefits, and death benefits.[3]

The SJSN Law was passed in 2004, and implementing legislation for insurance programmes was supposed to be passed by 2009. By 2010, the law that would allow execution of the policy by reorganizing the positions and responsibilities of insurance providers had still not been passed. The Yudhoyono government had kept deferring presentation of legislation. Finally, legislation emerged from the parliament itself, but still serious consideration of the bill was deferred.

The bill promised what amounted to an increase in the social wage that could improve the material conditions of many people, including union members. It was an issue with national implications, and could be addressed as such. A coalition of confederations, federations and other unions was formed, along with the NGO TURC, to campaign for the BPJS Bill to be passed. This was the Komite Aksi Jaminan Sosial (KAJS—Action Committee for Social Security). The term *Komite Aksi* immediately conjured up an image of the mobilizing committees that had mushroomed during the 1990s in opposition to the New Order. *Aksi* (mass action/street protest) was at the core of the strategy that forced Suharto from power. The KAJS was formally agreed upon at a meeting in Jakarta, 6–8 March 2010. The meeting was initiated by the FSPMI.[4] Other members included federations affiliated with the KPSI and KSBSI, as well as unaligned federations.[5] Said Iqbal, FSPMI president, was chosen as secretary-general of KAJS.

The goal of KAJS was to bring pressure on the parties in parliament to pass the BPJS Bill. Its use of 1990s *aksi* mobilization tactics was therefore not aimed at deepening radicalization but at providing support for the lobbying that the unions and TURC were doing. KAJS lobbied, met members of parliament and eventually also took the government to court, charging that it had failed to carry out its legal responsibilities by not passing legislation to enable the SJSN to be implemented.

However, the KAJS rallies were large and militant, with tens of thousands of workers being mobilized on several occasions, including at the parliament building. The FSPMI's members, spearheaded by the well-organized Garda Metal brigade, provided critical mass to ensure effective demonstrations at each point. The campaign broadened its appeal and outreach when it also received active support from one of the more socially critical PDIP members of parliament, Rieke Diah Pitaloka. Pitaloka was well known, having been a high-profile television personality before entering politics. Her electorate overlapped with the factory districts, and she built considerable popularity both for the campaign and for herself in those areas.

Lobbying, legal challenges and campaign mobilizations continued throughout 2010 and into 2011. On 11 October, following heightened campaigning and threats of further escalation, parliament finally passed the BPJS Bill. There remained criticism from civil society and from the left that the bill was not progressive enough, as its coverage was not total and that it also required payment of premiums. However, it was generally seen as a significant advance and as a victory for the KAJS and the unions.

This win increased the standing of the unions, especially the FSPMI, but also of the KSPI, of which it was the strongest member federation. It also set the precedent for a broad union coalition campaign, including mobilizations, to achieve change. It should be noted here, however, that the use of *aksi* mobilizations was not the core strategy but was a way to assist the lobbying and legal challenges that KAJS had been making. The KAJS used one of the methods of struggle of the 1990s radical political stream, but *not its strategy*. In the context of the time, this should not be surprising. The key unions involved did not come out of the 1990s dissident union stream, but out of the FSPSI constituency. The TURC was a research and education NGO that did indeed have links through association with the LBH to the ferment of the 1990s, but it was not an organization aimed at expanding, organizing and mobilizing a membership. Its focus was on policy formation, lobbying and legal advocacy. Its key leaders were lawyers.

By the end of 2011, the FSPMI (and thus to a large extent the KSPI) were consolidated, as were the KSPSI and others. The FSPMI/KSPI, however, had also gained experience in national campaign mobilizing and lobbying. In the aftermath of the BPJS campaign, there were two other issues that presented themselves as foci for campaigns. These issues agitated members across the country, including in the factory belts around Jakarta and in the city, as well as in all provinces. A large percentage of the expanded workforce was employed on a temporary basis, often through labour hire. This was called "outsourcing". Workers employed through "outsourcing" most likely received no sick pay, no holiday rights and no security of employment. They might also lose some of their wages to the labour hire agencies.[6] Outsourcing presented itself as an issue that could be taken up nationally by the big confederations.

The Indonesian minimum wage determination includes an annual review of what is considered an *upah layak* ("acceptable/ dignified wage level"), and minimum wage levels are then considered by a tripartite committee. The minimum wage is determined at the district level, with different rates in each region (and for different sectors). Assessments of the *upah layak* are made and submitted by the unions, employers and government, but the district governments make the final decision. Unions have always spoken out for significant wage increases every year.

The 2012 "National Strike"

The review of the minimum wage takes place towards the end of each year, starting around November, which meant, in 2012, almost exactly a year after the KAJS campaign ended. Consideration of a 2012 national action at the time of the review seems to have started soon after 11 October 2011, if indeed not beforehand. The period from late 2011 into 2012 was also marked by increased agitation among many workers around wages and employment status. Indonesian legislation banned companies from using "outsourcing" in the production process. It was legally permitted only in areas such as security guards, catering and some other work not directly linked to production.

Already in 2011, and then into 2012, there were an increasing number of protests by workers regarding wages, but also outsourcing. The first peak was in January 2012, when workers from hundreds of companies blocked the major Jakarta-Cikampek toll road, causing massive traffic problems and stopping economic activity in the area.[7] The toll road occupation by what the media reported as thousands of workers occurred following several earlier rallies and marches protesting the court appeal by the main employers' associations against the increase in the minimum wage agreed to by the West Java government. The wage increase was 15.9 per cent, and Apindo (Indonesian Employers Asscocation) was arguing for only a 5 per cent raise. The unions won the struggle and the 15.9 per cent increase was granted. Several unions were involved. The FSPMI in Bekasi, through a

Bekasi Workers Alliance, played a leading role. Its central Bekasi figure, Obon Tabroni, frequently acting as spokesperson.[8]

In the atmosphere stirred up by the KAJS campaign and the wave of protests that peaked in the mass toll road occupations in January 2012, it is not surprising that an increasing frequency of actions was reported in the following months. Moreover, the labour protest activity acquired a new aspect; namely, actions of solidarity. These were mobilizations from one or more factories to support strikes or pickets outside other factories.[9] This was no doubt facilitated by the fact that the federations and confederations had consolidated and had worked together, even if unevenly, in the KAJS campaign. The trend was strengthened by the factories being located close together in state industrial estate areas, which concentrated workers. Huge numbers of workers can be seen arriving and departing through the main gateways as shifts change. There was a material base for more interaction and solidarity between workers in different factories. The issues they faced—low wages and lack of job security due to outsourcing— were the same. They all faced anonymous employers, as factories were owned by people they never met.

The solidarity actions took on a very effective militant character as they became more than simple acts or statements of solidarity. From shows of support where existing disputes were visible, they became efforts to encourage workers to organize and campaign. These actions became known as *geruduk*, meaning to mass outside. Large district or estate-wide actions were known as "sweeping": workers would sweep through factory areas urging others to join them. This might include encouraging a strike or encouraging workers coming off shift to join demonstrations. This seems to have been a constant activity between at least May and October 2012. Delegate committees from the FSPMI were most active in carrying out *geruduk*. These actions during

2012 boosted the FSPMI's membership as it won over workers in unorganized factories or in other, less active, unions. According to FSPMI statistics, its membership in 2005 had reached 100,000. As it consolidated further, it had grown to 125,000 by 2010 and hovered around that number until the beginning of 2012. By February 2013 it had grown to 220,000[10]—it had grown by 100,000, almost doubling within a year. Some FSPMI officials directly attribute the growth to these *geruduk* actions.[11]

Earlier, in May 2012, another coalition was announced, the Majelis Pekerja Buruh Indonesia (MPBI—Indonesian Workers and Labourers' Assembly). The core members were the KSPSI and the KSPI. These two unions alone covered a big constituency. The KSPSI still retained the majority coverage of former FSPSI members, and inherited access to the largest number of factories. The KSPI was smaller, but it had shown its campaigning capacity and had coverage of factories with a strong bargaining position, such as in the large automobile plants, which would suffer major losses if production stopped. The MPBI announced that there would be a national strike (MONAS—"Mogok Nasional") later in the year, when the annual review of the minimum wage was to take place. The announcement was made at a May Day rally in the huge Istora Sports Stadium in Jakarta, with perhaps a hundred thousand workers filling the venue. The demands would be for wage rises, an end to outsourcing, and a proper start to the implementation of schemes under the BPJS Social Security Law.

Before looking at the course and results of the MONAS in October, it is necessary to emphasize the high level of activity that had begun in 2011, encouraged by the KAJS Social Security Bill campaign, and which continued through the first half of 2012. There had also been a well-publicized strike in West Papua at the Freeport mine. Union members in Jakarta were also very aware of the strikes that had taken place in other provinces. Probably the most militant were in the industrial estates of Batam Island, next to Singapore, in 2011.[12] The strikes on Batam involved tens of thousands of workers—defying a huge police presence that fired shots to try to quell the demonstrations—and completely closed down the factories and transportation there.[13]

The national strike of October did not come out of the blue, but was the product of a lengthy gestation. Furthermore, by 2011–12, there were economic and social factors also encouraging this process.

Fuelled by a sustained growth in commodity exports (minerals, timber), the economy had grown steadily, facilitating a ten-year-long growth in the middle class (i.e., those with a disposable income equivalent or better than that of a comfortable worker in an industrialized nation). Demand for cars, motorbikes, white goods and plasma televisions expanded rapidly. While there was no significant genuine industrialization,[14] the rapid expansion of assembly manufacture provided the base for a new, more consolidated and well-resourced unionism. Probably the most spectacular statistic that evidences this middle-class growth is the increase in motor car assembly. In 1997 annual car sales were 400,000, in 2005 they were 600,000, and in 2012 they were in excess of a million.[15] Sales of motorbikes, although a much less expensive item, have grown exponentially. Now workers in the large plants manufacturing car components, assembling cars, motorbikes, white goods, mobile phones and some mass-produced food products are playing a leading role.

As parts of the formal sector "boomed", this improved the bargaining position of unions. It provided a material base for their increased self-confidence. The unions, though a small section of the workforce, are concentrated in sectors that are most crucial to the economy's current activity. Many of these companies service the local market and are tied to Indonesia as a location for manufacture. So despite the unions' small size (relative to the workforce as a whole), they were in a stronger bargaining position.

However, such a boost in confidence and combativity is not a simple mechanistic product of the new manufacturing. Nor is it simply an automatic result of the consolidated unions entering into a new phase. Of course, in the new period in which union leaders were not backed by the state and were in competition with other unions, they did have to consider how to continue to deliver improvements to workers. Some would have been drawn into union activity with that ideal in mind.

The Nexus with Pre-1998 Radical Politics

It is clear also that conscious propagandizing for more militant and solidarity activities and careful tactical planning were crucial in the successes of 2011 and 2012. This education seems to have been initiated from within or near the FSPMI by activists from the pre-1998 radical political current. One of these was Danial Indrakusuma, mentioned above, a central figure in the PRD before 1998 who also played a key role in advocating the strategy of mass mobilizing.[16] He was one of a few people from or connected to that current who became central in the educational programmes accessed by FSPMI members and others. He was a popular figure among many workers who had been in his classes or read his ideas on union tactics during this period.[17] Since 2011 (at least), he has publicly advocated a new workers' party. He and others organized classes at an abandoned bridge in Bekasi, referred to as Rumah Buruh, as well as a house in another area, referred to as Saung Buruh. The first classes were held in the worker-occupied factory Kymko. Rumah Buruh educational activities were only semi-formally part of FSPMI activity.

In an article published in the labour affairs publication *Jurnal Sedane*, he throws some light on their activity.[18] Indrakusuma explains the factors he thinks led to the increased self-confidence of workers. In addition to the points above, he emphasizes the internal processes within the FSPMI and other unions. Among these was the involvement of workers in seminars carried out in conjunction with research-oriented NGOs, such as the Trade Union Rights Centre. This deepened the understanding of some workers of the wage system and, more crucially, the extent of "outsourcing" and the gap between the outsourcing situation and existing legislation. According to Indrakusuma, almost 80 per cent of workers carrying out central work in major plants are "outsourced", i.e., workers with a casual status hired through labour contractors.

He emphasized the high level of activity that had developed, referring to the toll road occupations, which, he related, occurred four times since 2011. He noted that the Jakarta Police Command recorded 957 *aksi* by workers during 2012, 725 of which it listed as being carried out by FSPMI-affiliated unions.

He described the policy of encouraging *rapat akbar* (mass meetings, though the Indonesian term conjures up the great anti-colonial mass meetings). These discussed strategy and tactics and were also a means of showing support for their demands. The holding of *vergadering*—mass meetings to discuss politics openly—was a key goal discussed by the PRD before 2007. These open meetings began in 2010 at the Kymko factory with hundreds and then up to 3,000 participants. This was followed by a mass meeting of 10,000 at Pilar Sports Stadium in Bekasi and later of 30,000 in a field in the Jurong industrial area in Bekasi. On May Day 2012 the MPBI unions organized an event in the main Jakarta sports stadium, with at least 60,000 present—this followed a rally of 100,000 earlier in the day.

Another factor, he argued, was due to the confidence-building presence of the Garda Metal (Metal Guard), a disciplined formation of the more physically prepared workers that often leads mobilizations and provides a sense of security. There is always a strong police presence, and sometimes a military one, at demonstrations. The Garda Metal also appears to be better trained, and reports directly to the union president; something which may turn out to have its own implications later on.

All these developments, including the emergence of Rumah Buruh and Saung Buruh as points of consolidation for the most combative elements, mean increasing numbers of this section of the union membership have been becoming better prepared for campaigning. Many factors were present for a large and effective mobilization.

In a press statement on 3 October 2012,[19] the newly formed MPBI stated that two million workers mobilized for the national "strike" it had called for that date, with mobilizations in factory belts (*kawasan industri*) or outside government offices in twenty-one cities and towns.

Press and social media reports separately estimated that hundreds of thousands of workers mobilized in Jakarta's industrial estates. Activists I talked to described the streets of the *kawasan industri* swarming with hundreds of thousands of workers. The media reported that tens of thousands of others gathered in Indonesia's larger cities and thousands in smaller towns. The mobilizations were scheduled to go for a few more days, but the MPBI leadership called them off after one day, following meetings with the minister for labour. The MPBI gave the government two weeks to come up with a satisfactory answer to its demands, or the strike would resume. The demands articulated by the MPBI, and supported by other unions—including the more overtly

left, but much smaller, Sekber Buruh (Workers' Secretariat)—
were for an increase in wages, an end to outsourcing, and the
full implementation of health insurance legislation to cover all
workers, with employers paying the premiums.

The fact that the Yudhoyono government resumed
negotiations with MPBI on the day of the strike indicated that
it was sensitive to the threat represented by ongoing worker
protests. Employer groups were protesting loudly from one end
of the country to the other in the lead-up to and on the day of
the strike. While editorials were often hostile, working journalists'
reports were generally sympathetic. The government was hard-
pressed to justify a situation in which employers used outsourced
workers illegally. This is harder when the ruling party, and most
of the state apparatus, is constantly embroiled in corruption
cases. The minister for economic affairs, Hatta Rajasa, came out
after the strike supporting the wage increase demanded by the
unions (from about US$140 per month to around US$175).[20] By
November 2012, increases in the official minimum wage of over
40 per cent were won.[21]

The actions were well reported in the media but had minimal
impact on the general political atmosphere because of the isolation
of most of the mobilizations in the factory belts outside the city
proper. The union demands—increases in the minimum wage and
an end to outsourcing—also have weak immediate relevance to
the 80 per cent of the workforce who are in the informal sector
and small enterprises.[22] However, the employers clearly felt the
wave of strikes. The Indonesian Business Association and its
head, Sofyan Wanandi, a prominent New Order figure, fought
the wage rises and attacks on outsourcing all through 2011 and
2012, including threatening factory closures. In November 2012,
the GERINDRA leader, Prabowo Subianto, chimed in opposing

the wage increases.[23] The minister of labour, Muhaiman Iskandar, the head of the Muslim National Awakening Party, also assisted businesses by instructing local governments to agree to delay the implementation of the minimum wage where small and medium enterprises professed hardship.

Backlash and Retreat

From late October 2012, anti-strike instructions were issued by district administrators, although they had no authority to do so. The police also made announcements backing this. This was followed by the emergence of an organization called the Masyarakat Bekasi Bergerak (Bekasi Society on the Move). Under the banner of this organization, large bands of *preman* (hoodlums) systematically harassed picket lines. They also attacked and burned down the Saung Buruh.

In fact, there had been regular physical clashes between *preman* groups and workers all through 2012, although some of these were not directly related to industrial disputation but were rather ongoing activity of the *preman* aimed at extorting money. In some cases, smaller groups of workers could be intimidated; in other cases, large fights took place. One such clash, on 29 October, manifested the strong relationship between the educational campaign and worker combativity. According to activists, and confirmed in many photos distributed through social media, ten thousand workers responded to news that the *preman* were going to attack the Rumah Buruh. Within a few hours, the workers arrived at the entrance on motorbikes, armed with pieces of wood and cane.[24] This mobilization did not need formal union instructions: workers mobilized spontaneously in defence of an institution—which has no official union status—they had come to value. In a clash on 19 November, workers tactically defeated the *preman*, who were unable to carry out the attack.[25]

Overall, while the MONAS won major wage increases, there were also signs of a hardening by employers. This created pressure that weakened union industrial campaigning.

An event on 8 November in Bekasi signalled a weakening of the momentum from the union officialdom. The centre of activity during 2012 in the factory belt outside Jakarta was Bekasi. Bekasi unions were a crucial motor of activity, so this event had a huge impact.

After a year of ongoing union mobilizations, winning very large wage increases, the momentum suddenly halted. On 8 November, representatives of the unions, the Bekasi business associations and the government, with police and army representatives also present, signed a Deklarasi Harmoni Industri Bekasi (Bekasi Industrial Harmony Declaration).[26] The declaration seemed to drop from the sky. It came very quickly, almost immediately, after the national strike. It became the framework in which *geruduk*, solidarity and sweeping started to be discouraged by the union leaderships.

The declaration contained six points. Although they were all formulated in very general terminology, it was clearly a declaration against conflict and militancy. The final points emphasized the need to create a climate in which enterprises could be productive and develop in a competitive environment. The emphasis was on consensus, cooperation and developing industrial relations in which all benefited. Much of the language was reminiscent of New Order industrial relations.

Representatives of the unions were Obon Tabroni, president of the Bekasi branch of the FSPMI; R. Abdullah, Bekasi head of the SPSI; Joko Tugimin, Bekasi president of the Serikat Pekerja Nasional (SPN—National Workers' Union); and Sepriyanto, Bekasi head of the Gabungan Serikat Pekerja Manufaktur Independen

Indonesia (GSPMII—Association of Indonesian Independent Manufacture Trade Unions). The two big unions, the FSPMI and the SPSI, were represented.

Employer representatives were Sutopo, head of the Bekasi branch of the Asosiasi Pengusaha Indonesia (Apindo); Dedi Wijaja, head of the West Java Apindo; Obing Fachruddin, head of the Bekasi Chamber of Commerce and Industry (Kadin); Sanny Iskandar, Bekasi head of the Himpunan Kawasan Industri Kabupaten Bekasi; and Deddy Harsono, chairperson of the Forum Investor Bekasi.

The declaration was also signed by the governor of West Java, Ahmad Heryawan, the *bupati* of Bekasi, Neneng Hasanah Yasin, as well as village heads, members of parliament and an Islamic community figure. Two military officers with the rank of colonel heading up local army commands also signed, as did the head of the Bekasi police.

Coming so quickly after the national strike, this was a remarkable turn-around. There were two key aspects to this change in trajectory. First was an ending of the connection with and input from all elements that were associated with the pre-1998 political currents, both the moderate lobby-oriented aspect, represented by TURC, and especially the more radical elements. This took a number of forms. First, union members were banned from attending the educational classes, called *ekopol*, that thousands had already attended. The classes were stopped. The large meetings of workers to discuss politics and economics at the Rumah Buruh and Saung Buruh stopped. The two key educators, Danial Indrakusuma and Sarinah, had their formal ties with the FSPMI ended in April 2013.[27]

This was a tightening of ideological control over the membership. There are no real public statements from the FSPMI officials explaining this ending of the *ekopol* or the later "expulsion" of Indrakusuma and Sarinah. English language classes conducted by an Australian activist sympathizer were also stopped.

This development has important implications for the relationship between the mainstream and more radical currents in the context of the legacy from the New Order. The New Order was characterized by an absence of ideological contestation, by the dominance of a formally decreed ideology, the adherence to which was enforced from above. It was not only *geruduk*, *aksi* and *solidaritas* that were part of the pre-1998 dissident current but also "ideology", encompassing both adhering to an understanding of how society worked and a strategy as to how it could be changed. This ideological aspect was a central feature of the PPB-PRD-SMID current, as well as some of the NGO networks that were also part of the opposition to the New Order.

The Declaration of Industrial Harmony began a retreat from ideological contestation. It also involved the union officialdom pressuring members to close down various discussion forums that groups of members had established. The tightening of ideological control was accompanied by a closing of ranks in defence of the officials.

A second aspect relates to the beginnings of a turn by the FSPMI, as the most active union, to electoral politics. Said Iqbal, the central leader of the FSPMI, had stood as a candidate for the Partai Keadilan Sejahtera (PKS—Justice and Welfare Party) in 2009 in the electorate of Riau. During 2013, signs emerged that the FSPMI/KSPI leadership was developing an electoral perspective. With the Declaration of Industrial Harmony and the consequent de-escalation of industrial campaigning, the winning of improvements for workers, especially at the government policy level, would have to come via another path. Lower profile industrial campaigning on a workplace-by-workplace basis would have less direct political impact. The unions had essentially given up the KAJS style of campaigning.

Policy in the electoral arena also revealed a disagreement between FSPMI leaders and Indrakusuma. In elections for the governor of West Java in February 2013, one of the candidates was Rieke Dia Pitaloka, who had campaigned with the unions on the BPJS Bill and with them against petrol price rises in October 2012. She stood as a PDIP candidate, with another pre-1998 NGO activist, Teten Masduki, as her running mate. Indrakusuma, citing this role and pointing to the advantages of broadening the union movement's campaigning, advocated support for her campaign. Indrakusuma also pointed to public promises made by the FSPMI leadership at earlier actions to support Pitaloka. While some individual members and at least one leader of the FSPMI leadership supported Rieke,[28] there was also de facto FSPMI support for the incumbent governor, Ahmad Heryawan, the KSPI secretary-general, attending a campaign event. It should be noted that Heryawan was a signatory to the Declaration of Industrial Harmony the previous October. He was also a member of the PKS, the same party for which Iqbal had stood in 2009. The PKS was also closely aligned with GERINDRA, a party established as a vehicle for Prabowo Subianto.

The fuller implications of the FSPMI and KSPI developing a serious electoral orientation became clear only later in 2013. During 2013 there were therefore two political processes that dominated the FSPMI/KSPI's planning: the carrying out of another national strike in October or November 2013, and preparing a more substantial electoral intervention.

Although it was never made clear publicly, it is not impossible that diverging electoral orientations played a role in the break-up of the MPBI, and of the cooperation between the KSPSI and KSPI. The KSPSI leadership's links were with the PDIP. They gave verbal support to the Pitaloka campaign. By March and April 2013, discussion around both the general elections and the presidential election scheduled for 2014 had begun. Given the developments between October 2012 and February 2014, including the Declaration of Industrial Harmony and the West Java gubernatorial election, it is not surprising that the two confederations were not able to continue the MPBI alliance.

This breakdown of the alliance meant that the annual national protests of 2013 were not organized by the MPBI but by a smaller coalition called the Konsolidasi Nasional Gerakan Buruh (KNGB—Labour Movement National Consolidation). The KNGB comprised the KSPI, the Workers Joint Secretariat (Sekber Buruh), KSN, and several other union federations and regional alliances. Meanwhile, the KSPSI aligned with the government, stating that it did not think significant rises in the minimum wage were justified. The KNGB had similar demands as in 2012: a 50 per cent rise in the minimum wage, the end of outsourcing, and the full application of the new health insurance law. They had won big wage rises in 2012, although many workers had still not received the increase, but there had been little progress in eliminating outsourcing. Improvements in the BPJS health system were not being widely felt.

On the first day of the strike in 2013, police noted actions in fifty towns and cities in fifteen provinces. It is difficult to assess how many workers took part—probably several hundred thousand. Activists report that in the industrial belts around Jakarta, production stopped in about forty per cent of factories, despite the abstention of the two large confederations. There was also systematic harassment, especially in the factory belts, by uniformed gangs, mostly belonging to the paramilitary Pemuda Pancasila (PP), an organization formed during the Suharto period. The PP and other groups mobilized to prevent workers leaving factory compounds or neighbourhoods to join mobilizations. In some cases there were physical attacks, resulting in workers being hospitalized with stab wounds. Later, there were clashes between organized workers and the PP and other similar groups. Police were often present but usually did nothing to stop the PP. In other areas, such as Sumatra and Sulawesi, police attacked protesters. On the factory island of Batam, it is reported that the factory belts were brought to a total halt.[29]

As preparations for the October-November mobilization unfolded, some of the constraints operating among the unions became clearer. First was the fact that two major confederations, KPSI and KSBSI, aligned with the government. But there was also a struggle over consciousness among the workers. The primary issue was the seriousness of having an actual strike. As discussions unfolded, including among Facebook groups, it was revealed that even in 2012, many "striking" workers were not really on strike. The huge mobilizations took place between shifts. While these were impressive shows of support and shocked employers, the fact was that most protesting workers did not stop production. In September-October, some militant workers, as well as activists, campaigned to convince workers to strike and that the best way to ensure this—in the face of a lack of seriousness from union leaders—was the increased use of the tactic of "sweeping", or *geruduk*. In practice, "sweeping" constituted a form of leadership from below by the most militant workers, going around and overtaking the official union leadership.

Consciousness in these new unions, at all levels of leadership and among the factory base, is very uneven. There is constant struggle over the best tactics and appropriate levels of militancy. The forty per cent strike rate militant activists estimated was a major gain, confirming for them the usefulness of leadership from below. It also strengthened the trend towards a differentiation within the unions and among membership, primarily at the base; a polarization that was pushed along by the reality that the 2013 round of protests failed to achieve the sought-for wage increases.

Role of Left Unions: Sekber Buruh

In the developments between 2010 and 2013, the interaction between the FSPSI stream and the dissident and radical union stream was that between individual activists from the dissident tradition, via both ex-PRD (Danial Indrakusuma) and the NGO wing (TURC). This interaction, in the form of either working within the union structure, as with Indrakusuma, or in close collaboration as a policy research advisor (TURC), was not the norm in relations between the two currents. This is especially the case for the organizations that evolved between 1998 and 2014 and which had strong ideological inclinations. These groups tended to organize and act separately from the large confederations. By 2010, the unions that had evolved and were associated with the various more left political groups formed their own alliance, the Sekretarian Bersama Buruh (Sekber Buruh). The core founding members were the PRP, KPO-PRP and PPI. Student organizations joined as well as unions. Sekber issued joint statements and, sometimes, for major mobilizations, held joint actions, such as for May Day and on the occasion of the 2012 MONAS. The Sekber unions also always mobilized on days of national mobilization called by the large confederations, including 2012. However, their actions were organized separately. On some occasions there could even be tensions between the confederation unions and Sekber unions in the field.

The interaction with the FSPMI by Indrakusuma and those working with him represented a major departure from past practice by the more left, small unions. During the 1990s, the PPBI had been an integral part of the PPBI-PRD-SMID nexus and was seen as being closely aligned with the PRD. After 1998, as more left-oriented groups emerged, either out of the PRD or independently, they also organized unions that were aligned with their blocs. There were no serious cases of left groups working within the existing large confederations. In the 1990s, of course, working within the FSPSI would have been neither possible nor effective, given the nature of the FSPSI as an arm of state power. However, after 1998, as the terrain changed and new confederations, federations and unions developed, the large confederations were not arms of state power. This did not mean that the political outlook of their leaderships radicalized to the left, but it did mean that they had to have policies to win some improvements for their members. In the period 2007–14, the very close interaction with the FSPMI by Indrakusuma and others could be viewed as experimentation—albeit with tiny forces and resources—in a new method. There were tensions between Indrakusuma and Sekber activists, even those historically most close to Indrakusuma, regarding these different approaches.

However, after 2012 the trend has been towards a reversal of this situation. Heading towards elections in early 2014, the MPBI alliance between the KSPSI and the KPSI broke down. When the MPBI broke down, the KSPI/FSPMI agreed to a new alliance to organize the 2013 MONAS. This was the KNGB, which comprised the KSPSI/FSPMI and Sekber. The formation of the KNGB did not add any serious mobilizing power because the Sekber unions were all relatively small—tiny in comparison to the KSPSI's formal membership and the KSPI's membership, which also had a large active component. The largest of the unions coming out of the 1990s dissident stream, KASBI, did not join KNGB but still mobilized on the MONAS dates. However, the formation of the KNGB did allow the 2013 MONAS to be portrayed as the mobilizations of an alliance, not just a single confederation. As indicated above, the KSPI was already moving in a conservative direction. The cooperation between the Sekber unions and the KSPI/FSPMI in the lead-up to MONAS 2013 would eventually lead to a division among the left groups, although this took a year to develop.

The 2013 MONAS did not have the same impact as in 2012, despite the appearance of a broader coalition. The coalition was broader in the sense of the political spectrum that was represented, but narrower in terms of the numbers of union members represented.

Notes

1. A general picture of the activities of these unions can be obtained from the websites, Facebook pages and groups and media coverage. For an early 2011 review of worker protest activity, see Benny Hari Juliawan, "Street-level Politics: Labour Protests in Post-authoritarian Indonesia", *Journal of Contemporary Asia* 41, no. 3 (2011): 349–70. For a view on the KAJS and related campaign activity, see Abu Mufakhir, "Alliances of Labour Unions as the Backbone of General Strikes in Indonesia", in *Resistance on the Continent of Labour Strategies and Initiatives of Labour Organizing in Asia*, edited by Fahmi Panimbang (Asia Monitor Resource Centre, 2017). The title of this article is somewhat misleading as there have been no "general strikes" in Indonesia. The author is basically referring to larger than normal strikes, involving more than one factory, and not a general strike in the normal sense.

2. Surya Candra, "The Indonesian Trade Union Movement a Clash of Paradigms", in *Worker Activism after Reformasi 1998: A New Phase for Indonesian Unions?*, edited by Jafar Suryomenggolo (Asia Monitor Resource Centre, 2014).

3. Ibid.

4. Ibid., p. 48.

5. For a complete list, see ibid., p. 49.

6. See Zely Ariane, "A New Wave of Workers Struggles in Indonesia", September 2012, http://www.asia-pacific-solidarity.net/asiapacific/focus/zely_anewwaveofworkersstruggle_130912.htm.

7. "West Java Increases Minimum Wage Levels by 25 Percent", *Jakarta Globe*, 22 November 2012.

8. http://www.antaranews.com/berita/294749/buruh-bekasi-dan-apindo-berunding.

9. Danial Indrakusuma, "Rachmat, Tarikh (Sejarah), Hidayah dan Rekomendasi", https://www.facebook.com/notes/danial-indrakusuma/rachmat-tarikh-sejarah-hidayah-dan-rekomendasi/10152100952453538/.

10. David Duncan, "Out of the Factory, Onto the Streets: The Indonesian Metalworkers Union Federation (FSPMI) as a Case of Union Revitalisation in Indonesia" (BA Hons. thesis, 2015), p. 207.

11. Duncan, ibid., quotes such interviews.

12. "Government Vows to Protect Businesses from Anarchic Rallies", *Jakarta Post*, 5 November 2015.

13. "Security Guards, Soldiers Beat Workers, Start Batam Riot: Witness", *Straits Times*, 21 September 2011.

14. By which I mean no steel or capital goods manufacturing capacity, and no extensive mass production using machinery, but rather widespread tool-based production, as exemplified by the data on enterprise size. Daniel Bellefleur, Zahra Murad, and Patrick Tangkau, "A Snapshot of Indonesian Entrepreneurship and Micro, Small, and Medium Sized Enterprise Development", US AID, https://crawford.anu.edu.au/acde/ip/pdf/lpem/2012/20120507-SMERU-Dan-Thomson-Bellefleur.pdf.

15. Car sales dropped in 2014 and 2015 but reached more than a million again in 2016–17. https://www.indonesia-investments.com/id/business/business-columns/automotive-industry-news-sgmw-motor-indonesia-enters-car-market/item7976.

16. For a key article by Indrakusuma on mass action strategy and tactics, see his "Sang Panda Api", in *Liber Amicorum 80 Tahun Joesoef Isak*,

edited by Max Lane and Bonnie Triyana (ISAI, Komunitas Bambu, Perkumpulan Praxis, 2008).

17. Indrakusuma's Facebook account has 5,000 friends and almost 10,000 followers. It appears most of these are from the union milieu.

18. Danial Indrakusuma, "Rachmat, Tarikh (Sejarah), Hidayah dan Rekomendasi", https://www.facebook.com/notes/danial-indrakusuma/rachmat-tarikh-sejarah-hidayah-dan-rekomendasi/10152100952453538/.

19. "Workers Plan Strike in Protest against Salary and Outsourcing", *Jakarta Post*, 3 October 2012.

20. http://surabaya.tribunnews.com/m/index.php/2012/10/11/hatta-rajasa-upah-buruh-rp-15-juta-tidak-cukup.

21. http://kusmoro.wordpress.com/2011/12/02/upah-minimum-kabupaten-kota-bekasi-2012/.

22. I use the term "informal proletarians" rather than "urban poor" or "informal sector". The daily sociological experience of the informal proletarian can create different kinds of more eclectic thinking and psychology—and present problems for organizing—among these masses compared to those working in the larger factories and other workplaces. Still, however complicated the mediating linkages may be, these masses survive (reproduce themselves within a capitalist framework) and, in one form or another, their survival depends on their being able to sell their labour power. They are proletarians in a system made up primarily of bourgeois and proletarians.

23. http://finance.detik.com/read/2012/12/18/142130/2121436/4/prabowo-sentil-buruh-jangan-minta-gaji-naik-terlalu-tinggi.

24. There are very clear photographs of this mobilization. Some show the streams of workers on motorbikes arriving near the Rumah Buruh bridge. Others show the thousands of workers, many carrying pieces of wood, assembled in front of the bridge. Most of these photographs have been uploaded on to Facebook.

25. http://spai-fspmi.or.id/editorial-perjuangan-pembentukan-serikat-di-samsung/and also http://spai-fspmi.or.id/serikat-buruh-samsung-dipasung/.

26. *Kompas*, 8 November 2012, http://megapolitan.kompas.com/read/2012/11/08/17052399/Deklarasi.Harmoni.Industri.Bekasi.Didukung.

27. Communication with Indrakusuma.

28. FSPMI activist Nyumarno supported Rieke, as did Obon Tabrani. The FSPMI and Iqbal initially also supported Pitaloka, proposing Obon Tabrani as a candidate for deputy governor. However, this did not eventuate, and Teten Masduki became her running mate. http://nasional.kompas.com/read/2012/11/04/17454594/Buruh.Calonkan.Obon.Tabroni; https://www.facebook.com/permalink.php?story_fbid=428393333970280&id=419044968238450&comment_tracking=%7B%22tn%22%3A%22O%22%7D.

29. "Massive Strike Nearly Cripples Industries in Batam", *Jakarta Post*, 1 November 2013.

Chapter 4

The Labour Movement and "Go Politics"

By early 2013—or even by the time of the Declaration of Industrial Harmony—the KSPI/FSPMI, under the leadership of Said Iqbal, appeared to be preparing for greater involvement in electoral politics. This was not a turn from apolitical unionism to political unionism, as some have argued,[1] as Indonesian unions have always been intensely political. This was the case under the New Order when the FSPSI was integrated into the political system and campaigns supporting the New Order. It was the case with the unions after 1998, whose leaders either sought connections with political parties or engaged in lobbying and campaigning to influence government policy and legislative outcomes through the parliament. The new trajectory that became increasingly clear throughout 2013 and into 2014 was characterized by a systematic attempt to increase direct representation of the KSPSI/FSPMI in legislative bodies and later in executive positions, as well as a conscious alignment with a specific political bloc and perspective as, I will argue, *a substitute for increasing the militancy and breadth of industrial campaigning*—and not as its complement.

These developments since 2013—called by the union itself "Go Politik!"—were not the FSPMI's first experimentation with electoral politics. In 2009, FSPMI members, with national leadership approval, stood for several different parties in the province of Kepulauan Riau, including for the municipal council in the city of Batam. This was a reversal of union policy on electoral participation that occurred after a change in national leadership, that is, when Said Iqbal replaced Thamrin Mossi as president of the FSPMI in November 2006. According to Ford,[2] there had been considerable discussion and efforts on the electoral front in Batam as early as 2004 and intense discussion in the national leadership.

The way in which FSPMI and other union members became candidates was very messy. There was an unofficial organization of FSPMI members in Batam, Jas Metal, who had been lobbying on this issue for some time. Some candidates had Jas Metal support, some put themselves forward without any organized backing. Other candidates were on a list issued by the FSPMI national leadership, which included Said Iqbal himself. As candidates for national, provincial or national parliaments needed to be on party lists, the union, Jas Metal and union members entered into talks with a range of parties.

Some, such as Said Iqbal, stood under the banner of the Partai Keadilan Sejahtera, a party with a strong Islamic orientation. Others, after various negotiations, stood under two other Islamic parties, the United Development Party (PPP—Partai Persatuan Pembangunan) and the National Mandate Party (PAN—Partai Amanat Nasional). There were also candidates who stood under the banners of nationalist and secular parties. There is not yet clear data on what actually determined why particular union members aligned with different parties, although in at least two cases Ford cites promises to provide a building for the union secretariat.

It is probable that ideology and general programmatic issues were not determinant for most. However, Ford does quote Said Iqbal as stating that he felt politically close to the PKS, although denying he was a member. In any case, no FSPMI or union member was elected. This is not surprising. The FSPMI members had no particular political or ideological identity beyond their immediate milieu. This was manifested in the apparent ease of campaigning under any party banner. Entering the electoral arena on that basis meant they were relying only on their identity as workers and union members to attract votes. There was no basis in previous experience to think this would work. It also assumes a generalized political authority for trade unions, which has not yet been established.

'Go Politics'—But in a Particular Direction

It was a full five years later that a more elaborated "Go Politics!" strategy emerged. The full context of the discussions that led in this direction is not clear. We can note that after Said Iqbal became president, the FSPMI became more open to electoral participation and, indeed, Iqbal had stood as a candidate himself. We should also note that the 2009 experiment indicated the limitations of such interventions by FSPMI. We can note also the support for Ahmed Heryanto rather than Pitaloka at the beginning of 2013.

In October 2012 the idea was again floated of a Partai Buruh (Workers Party) from Indrakusuma, who had been close to the FSPMI and its leadership. He raised the idea in an extensive interview with the labour publication *Jurnal Sedane*. It gained some traction briefly in the mainstream newspapers.[3] It appears that the issue of the unions, spearheaded by FSPMI, establishing a political party was being discussed at a leadership level.

The establishment of their own party did not, however, eventuate. It did not emerge as a topic for open discussion by the FSPMI leadership until after the presidential election in 2014, and then only inconsistently. The "Go Politics!" strategy in 2013 was similar to that pursued in 2009, except more centralized. Nine FSPMI officials were selected and negotiations conducted to have them accepted on the party lists of five different parties. Five stood as candidates for the Bekasi district parliament. Initially there was a proposal to hold elections within the union to select candidates, but this did not happen and the leadership appointed the candidates. The leadership argued that they had no time to carry out elections.[4]

Candidates stood for the following parties: PKS, PAN, GOLKAR, and PDIP. FSPMI officials emphasized, when interviewed, that a guiding principle was that there should be no "money politics" between the FSPMI and its candidates and the parties. They campaigned as much as possible as an FSPMI team, trying to distinguish themselves from the parties they were standing for. Election posters depicted all candidates, no matter what party they stood for, wearing the FSPMI uniform. Given that Indonesian elections, and Indonesian national politics in general, are still dominated by parties and their "identities", however empty, it is not surprising that their votes were low. Furthermore, it needs to be remembered that some of the parties themselves also had a record of relating to the trade unions' campaigns. The PDIP candidate was Rieke Pitaloka, who easily scored a large number of votes as a candidate in the national elections from the Bekasi district.[5]

In no case were the FSPMI candidates high on the list of candidates, meaning that they would be dependent on personal following due to their FSPMI position or overflow votes from the parties they were standing for. Again, as with the Batam experiment, there was no resistance from the FSPMI regarding putting candidates in a variety of parties; indeed, it was their proposal. Ideological, political or other differences between the parties (assuming they actually existed) were not an issue. Both in Batam and in the 2014 elections, the aim was simply to get somebody elected somewhere. This appears quite estranged from any idea of establishing a workers or labour party with an ideological and political identity of its own. Campaign billboards and other electoral material did downplay party identity while emphasizing union identity, but this was done pictorially, with posters showing candidates in FSPMI uniform, not through the promotion of any specific ideological or programmatic perspective.

According to Amalinda Savarini,[6] 27,483 people in a voting population of just over two million voted for candidates from the FSPMI in Bekasi, while the FSPMI membership in the area was 82,457. Only 33 per cent voted along union lines. In a situation where union structures and memberships are all relatively new and exist in a situation of competing unions as well as competing parties, there is no reason to assume that FSPMI members will vote for FSPMI candidates, or that workers will vote for candidates who emphasize their membership of a particular union. Indeed, what has been called a "zigzag" strategy may have made the candidates less distinguishable as they entered a party competition with no clear party loyalties. They were not standing as independent candidates in their own right—something which did not happen until 2017.

Two candidates were elected to the Bekasi district council, but neither actually received the required quota—they relied on overflow votes from their party lists. They were Nyumarno, who stood for the PDIP and had long been associated with the PDIP and Pitaloka's earlier campaigns, and Nurdin, who stood for PAN.

Overall, it would be difficult to argue that the FSPMI was able to establish itself as a significant electoral force in Bekasi, and certainly not nationally.

Perhaps anticipating the FSPMI's political limitations as later revealed by the parliamentary and district elections, and already revealed in Riau and Batam, the next phase of "Go Politik!" took on a new angle. Rather than appearing ideologically and politically indiscriminate in choosing parties, the FSPMI leadership began to take a clear stance on who it would support in the presidential elections, also scheduled for 2014.

During late 2013, especially after the October-November MONAS protests, Iqbal began making statements that he supported Prabowo Subianto for president. Prabowo was a controversial candidate in that many people considered him involved in human rights abuses during the New Order period. Iqbal made statements on and off during late 2013, but by early 2014 it had become clear that the KSPI/FSPMI were coming out in full support of Prabowo. At the same time, the KSPSI and the KSBSI were supporting Joko Widodo.

On 1 May 2014, at the Istora Stadium in front of a large (but not huge) crowd, Said Iqbal declared support for Prabowo, and Prabowo was invited to speak. At the May Day rally, Prabowo stated that he would sign on the spot a ten-point declaration of workers' demands (although he left, forgetting to do so). The FSPMI leadership, especially Iqbal, campaigned strongly for Prabowo, and also more openly associated itself with Prabowo's party, GERINDRA, frequently meeting GERINDRA leaders, such as Fadli Zon. There were also hints that in a Prabowo government, Iqbal would become minister of labour.

There are easily identifiable consistencies in this decision, such as the fact that Iqbal stood for PKS in 2009 and that the PKS was GERINDRA's most solid ally in 2014 and up until now. The

West Java FSPMI's support for a PKS candidate in 2013 is another example. However, the situation was (and is) probably more ambiguous than a simple imposition of a political line by Iqbal, although assessing the overall situation remains difficult because most decisions are made behind closed doors. Other factors can be identified that also make the situation more ambiguous. First, there are the signs of an earlier interest in starting a separate workers' party. There was the earlier support for Pitaloka during the KAJS campaign. There was, indeed, the interaction with Indrakusuma and TURC during 2010–13.

So a precise analysis of the motives and reasons for this sudden and very strong support for Prabowo remains difficult. However, from 2014 until today, this alignment has continued, despite there also having been an independent electoral campaign by Obon Tabrani in 2017.

The most recent manifestation[7] has been the electoral positioning of the FSPMI regarding the 2017 Jakarta gubernatorial election. During this period, the FSPMI leadership—usually through Iqbal, but also through Jakarta FSPMI leaders—consistently backed the candidates, Anies Baswedan and Sandiago, who were being supported by Prabowo's GERINDRA and the PKS.

Further, the KSPI/FSPMI fused its annual wage campaign in late 2016 with a conservative Islamic demonstration calling for the arrest of the PDIP candidate (see below).

2014–15 Industrial Campaigning

As I have emphasized, there are very many unions in Indonesia, not united under any one umbrella. News media reported workplace industrial protests, and occasionally at a local or even national level, by many unions throughout 2014–15. Given the number of unions involved and the uneven reporting of such activities, it is hard to provide an overall picture. It is possible to affirm, however, that the only mobilizations that registered as national political events were the annual mobilizations when minimum wage decisions were made.

It is easier to assess the 2014 and 2015 national mobilizations at the time of the minimum wage decision because these are well-publicized events that also have had a very visible history since 2010. Again, an assessment of those actions will focus on the most politically profiled unions, the KSPI and its member federation, the FSPMI, even when other unions joined in.

In this context, we can note the increasing integration of KSPI and FSPMI's industrial campaigning with electoral support for General Prabowo. The demands of the confederation remained more or less the same as before, but the activities became more electorally partisan. This is perhaps clearest in the early lead-up to the 2014 mobilizations. These began as usual with the May Day events, which were followed by a long march from Bandung to Jakarta.

At both May Day and in the publicity for the long march, the KSPI/FSPMI presented a basic list of ten demands, which became known as the Sepultura (Sepuluh Tuntutan Rakyat—Ten Demands of the People).[8] These were:

1. Increase the purchasing power of the workers and society's minimum wage by increasing the basket of goods used to determine the Decent Living Needs Index (KHL) from 60 to 84 goods and services as well as increasing workers' productivity.
2. End the policy of allowing the payment of the minimum wage to be postponed.
3. Implement the policy of guaranteed pensions for workers from 1 July 2015, in accord with the SJSN and BPJS Law.

4. Improve health insurance, granting free health services to workers and people with low incomes.

5. End outsourcing, including in BUMN (state-owned companies), and make all such workers permanent employees.

6. Pass the Bill on Domestic Workers and revise Labour Law No. 39/2004 to be more oriented to protecting migrant workers, and also pass the Bill on Nurses.

7. Repeal the Law on Mass Organizations and replace it with a law on associations.

8. Appoint honorary teachers and other workers as full civil servants and provide a million rupiah per month subsidy for them from the national budget.

9. Implement twelve years of compulsory schooling.

10. Allocate budget funds for scholarships for talented children of workers, up to tertiary level; provide cheap public transport and housing.

These ten demands reflected a consensus among most unions as to what a set of basic demands should be. Missing is a demand for a specific wage increase. Wage increases are covered in the demand for an expansion of the budget of goods used to calculate a minimum decent wage. While these demands do not represent a retreat on any earlier package of demands—except that there is no definitive wage increase demand—the May Day event did exhibit a new political orientation. Up until 2014, the May Day gatherings organized by the KPSI, whether via the MPBI in 2012 or the KNGB in 2013, had been a specific part of the unions' wages campaign. In 2014 it was turned into a rally in support of the presidential candidacy of General Prabowo.[9] This alignment had already brought with it a change in the character of the KSPI's political propaganda. As early as late 2013, Iqbal had already made statements that human rights were not relevant to workers in response to direct challenges as to why he was supporting a candidate whose human rights record was not considered positive by many.

The May Day assembly in the Istora Sports Stadium was followed later in June by a long march of KSPI members from Bandung to Jakarta. This action was also projected as part of the campaign in support of Prabowo's election. The event started on 10 June, one month before the July presidential election, and was described by the FSPMI as "an event to socialize the Sepultura as well as give support to candidates Prabowo – Hatta". The major Indonesian daily *Kompas* also published reports directly associating the FSPMI's Sepultura with its campaign for Prabowo, with headlines such as "This is the Sepultura which Prabowo is promising."[10]

The October mobilizations did take place.[11] However, from the start they had a different political character and less momentum behind them. Occurring just a few months after the presidential election, they were taking place in an atmosphere of widespread hope in a government that would be more oriented towards social welfare under the new president, Joko Widodo. Furthermore, while there had been ongoing industrial actions during the year by many unions, the large May and June events had already been subordinated to the needs of the political opposition to Widodo. Confusing this situation was an agreement that the 2014 mobilizations be carried out again in an alliance with the KSPSI and KSBSI, which had both supported Joko Widodo's candidacy.

While the union leadership had promised mobilizations of 1–3 million workers in 2011 and 2012, in 2014 Iqbal stated that the nationwide mobilization would be 100,000, with only 50,000 coming from the Jakarta area. He stated that there would be demonstrations in central Jakarta, but there was no mention of the usual mobilizations that had previously occurred in Tangerang and Karawang.

Newspapers reported the 2 October demonstrations as in the "thousands". Iqbal was quoted as demanding a 30 per cent increase in wages in Jakarta, starting in 2015. This followed the 44 per cent rise in 2013 and 10 per cent in 2014. The eventual increase approved by the Jakarta government, under Governor Basuki Cahaya Purnomo, was 12 per cent, taking the minimum to 2.7 million rupiah. The wage increases around the country were all in that modest range. The lower-than-expected wage increase resulted in a string of further protests during November and December, including by the KSPSI. It was clear that union leaderships could not just end the campaign as they had done in 2013 with the Harmony Declaration, as expectations among members were high. However, these demonstrations after the fact had no impact, and the momentum eventually faded. They presaged a more serious defeat for the unions in 2015.

The annual minimum wage mobilization in 2015 was initially announced to take place over eight days, 12–20 November, but was later postponed and shortened to take place over four days, 24–27 November. While there was also a May Day event, this seemed to win less of a political profile than in earlier years, except that it generated some discussion around the idea of a labour party—a topic that will be further discussed below. On the whole, 2015 was similar to the previous years, with media reports of ongoing workplace activities over wages, conditions and dismissals.

Politically, the focus emerged as controversy developed around a new government regulation that would change the way the annual minimum wage calculation was carried out.[12] Government Regulation 78/2015, which came into effect on 23 October, set the annual wage increase based on the inflation rate and economic growth. Using this formula, wage increases for 2016 were set at no more than 11.5 per cent. This regulation meant that there would be no more annual survey of the *kebutuhan hidup layak.* The assessment of the KHL, with business, union and government submissions, had been the basis for negotiations and decisions on all previous occasions. The new regulation now scheduled such assessments on a five-yearly basis. The new system meant that there would be no more formal basis for annual wage negotiations. The Widodo government had clearly decided to implement a major disempowering of trade unions.

The unions rejected this new approach. On 17 October, soon after the discussion around the new regulation became more public, KSPI chairman Said Iqbal told the *Jakarta Post* that all labour unions rejected the new formula.[13] He stated: "We urge the government to stop formulating the draft of a government regulation on wages. Let us—labour unions, business associations and the government's representatives—sit together to decide the formula for the 2016 minimum wage increase."

The government's insistence on the new regulation provoked a number of demonstrations outside parliament and also the presidential palace, especially in October and into November. The demonstrations are reported as having been carried out separately by the KSPSI, KSPI, KASBI and KSBSI. By May Day of 2015 a new coalition had also been established comprising some unions formerly associated with Sekber Buruh and KSPI. This was called the Gerakan Buruh Indonesia (GBI—Indonesian Workers' Movement) and was associated with calls for a labour party. Some of the protest actions were associated with GBI. This meant that most actions by these left unions were subsumed into the several actions of the larger confederations.

Most of these actions involved either hundreds or a few thousand workers. At one action organized by the KSPI in October, some scuffles occurred between police and workers and some workers were detained briefly, while the secretary-general of the KSPI was charged with an offence. As of mid-2016 that case had not proceeded to court.

There were also smaller but well coordinated actions carried out by the Komite Persatuan Rakyat (KPR—People's United Committee), a temporary coalition of smaller unions, student groups and activist committees, connected to activists who had taken an oppositional stance towards the KSPI leadership after its alignment with General Prabowo. These actions took place in Jakarta, Bekasi, Karawang and Purwakarta, but also in such places as Ternate and Medan. This appears to be an early attempt to construct an alternative pole of attraction to the mainstream confederations, including the KSPI.

Although the KPR was a temporary formation, it confirmed a bifurcation occurring in the union current that had emerged from the more radical dissident unions of pre-1998. A majority from the Sekber Buruh had joined the GBI with the KSPI/FSPMI. A small minority, in particular the Independent Workers' Solidarity Movement (GSBM) and the Federasi Serikat Buruh Demokratik Kerakyatan (F-SEDAR—Popular Democratic Union Federation), both linked to a political group in which Indrakusuma is involved, and workers supportive of solidaritas.net, opted to build a stream openly opposing the politics of the KSPI/FSPMI.

Mobilizations did take place on 24–27 November in Jakarta and other towns. However, they lacked the momentum and size of earlier years, especially 2011 and 2012, and even 2013. In some provinces governors increased wages slightly above the 11.5 per cent mandated by the new Regulation 78/2015, but the regulation has been maintained despite the protests. The removal of a formal basis for annual wage negotiations was a major defeat for the unions. Even in the KSPI's Sepultura, one demand was an increase in the basket of goods that determined the annual KHL amount. Now that became almost pointless, being reduced to something that happens only every five years.

The failure to budge the government on Regulation 78/2015 did not end union opposition to it. The KSPI lodged a judicial review case against the regulation in December 2015. Protest actions continued up until 2017. However, to date there has been no movement by the government to retreat from this regulation. On May Day 2016, the minister of labour made a point of affirming that the regulation would not be withdrawn.

Meanwhile, the opposition to the regulation through the KSPI became part of an opposition to the Widodo government in the framework of the KSPI alignment with General Prabowo's GERINDRA-PKS coalition.

This merging was most stark during the lead-up to the Jakarta gubernatorial elections. President Widodo's preferred candidate, nominated by his party, the PDIP, was Basuki Purnama Cahyono (Ahok). The GERINDRA-PKS alliance nominated a rival candidate, Anies Baswedan, and the KSPI/FSPMI campaigned for Baswedan. The KSPI's campaign involved a merging of the industrial and electoral campaigning in which the industrial campaigning was submerged. The clearest example of this was the union's merging of the annual minimum wage mobilization with the *Bela Islam* (Defend Islam) demonstration of 2 December 2016, whose main demand was the arrest of candidate Ahok on the grounds he had made demeaning statements about Islam. Baswedan and Prabowo had associated themselves with the leadership of this campaign. The KSPI had also already held actions against Governor Ahok, accusing him of corruption, and also opposing a major development project being implemented by him involving reclamation in Jakarta bay.

The union leaders claimed that their campaign was not simply piggybacking on the *Aksi Bela Islam* demonstrations, citing as evidence that a Google search of keywords relating to wages and national strike prior to 2 December showed higher figures than a search on the term "Bela Islam". They also cited the fact that the minister of labour had urged unions not to join the demonstration as evidence that their "enemy" was afraid of the tactic. At a meeting with workers on 1 December, as reported by *Koran Perjoeangan*, Said Iqbal reminded them that they shared some of the demands of *Bela Islam* in relation to their opposition to Ahok. He stated that even before the case of Ahok demeaning Islam, they had been protesting against the governor on other issues.[14]

The 2 December *Bela Islam* demonstration, demanding the arrest of Ahok, was very large, attended by probably between 200,000 and 300,000 people, although its organizers claimed that it had participation in the millions. It escalated the polemics around the "demeaning of Islam" and strengthened the Baswedan campaign. The issues of wages and conditions and opposition to Regulation 78/2015 were swamped in the media by the issues of sectarianism and Islam versus secular politics.

Baswedan himself initially took unclear positions on 78/2015. As early as October, when Governor Purnama increased the Jakarta minimum wage to 3,355,750 rupiah based on 78/2015, Baswedan restricted himself to saying that regulation and related issues would have to be "studied". He also emphasized reducing prices rather than increasing wages as the way to help wage earners. Later he signed a "political contract" with a coalition of Jakarta unions and federations in which he stated he would increase wages more than stipulated by 78/2015, taking into account price rises. There were no details on how much, how that would be calculated, or how, as governor, he would be able to defy national policy that had the force of government regulation.[15]

In fact, the "political contract" reads as the unions' ambit list of demands rather than a list of policies that Baswedan would be able to or willing to implement. The full list is:

1. A Jakarta decent wage level (not using PP 78/2015).
2. End outsourcing in Jakarta.
3. Cheap housing for workers.
4. Guaranteed free healthcare.
5. Guaranteed pensions for all Jakarta workers.
6. Make honorary teachers full public servants.
7. Cheap transportation.
8. Reject reclamation and evictions.
9. Reject revisions to Labor Law UU 13/2003.
10. Compulsory twelve years of schooling and scholarships for higher education.

This is virtually the same list as contained in the Sepultura that Prabowo agreed to before the presidential election.

Baswedan won the second round of elections against Purnama in April 2017 and is now governor. A test of the effectiveness of the KSPI's alignment with GERINDRA and PKS will be whether he offers serious resistance to the national government regarding Regulation 78/2015.[16]

'Go Politics'—Where Next?

At a seminar organized by TURC in 2012, a staff member gave an enthusiastic presentation on the history and policies of the Brazilian Workers' Party, holding it out as a possible model for a labour party in Indonesia. The presenter also outlined the gains in welfare policies under a Workers' Party government. The participants were union activists from around Indonesia, many from the FSPMI. One participant stated that the leadership of the FSPMI had asked for readings about the Brazilian party. It was in this early period—2011 to 2012—that the first public discussion occurred on the possibility of forming a labour party. This was a period of escalating campaigning. The SBSI union leader, Muchtar Pakpahan, had already launched a party in 1999, but that was a time when the new union landscape had not yet evolved, and only Pakpahan's union—also fragile as a later split showed—could be its basis.

As early as 2011, TURC had hosted a seminar at which a labour party had been advocated. This seminar was reported in the daily media, *Kompas* newspaper's 4 May report being entitled: "Kaum Buruh Sebaiknya Bentuk Parpol" ("Workers Should Form their own Party").[17] The reporter noted that the seminar was attended by Surya Candra (a leader of TURC and a labour lawyer who played a leading role in the KAJS), Muchtar Pakpahan and Danial Indrakusuma.

There was no organized or systematic discussion of the idea, with different actors making separate comments on the issue. TURC's seminars on the Brazilian Workers Party indicated that it was favourably disposed to such a development. Indrakusuma also gave an interview to the labour magazine *Jurnal Sedane* advocating for workers, through their unions, to establish a labour party.

Indrakusuma stated:

> Unions must make their own political party. It is a legitimate tactic to work via other parties, but it creates difficulties and you must have the mechanisms to deal with the side effects.... There are many vested interests working inside the parties you work in. Furthermore, none of them have a history of struggle

or of caring deeply about the people. And if they do struggle,
it is just pretense. Quite shameful. It should be like Brazil here:
the workers should have their own party with anti-neoliberal
policies on some things. The conditions here make such a
prospect feasible.[18]

Given the comments of union participants at the TURC seminar,
it is likely that the idea was already being discussed among
at least some of the FSPMI leadership. Perhaps the first clear
published statements on the issue were those on the FSPMI
website in April 2014, when Iqbal, on behalf of the FSPMI and
KSPI, supported the idea of a labour party, a stance which he
continues to affirm today, while at the same time advocating
support for GERINDRA-PKS candidates. In local elections in
2017, the FSPMI also supported a campaign by another FSPMI
official, Obron Tambrani, as an independent candidate for *bupati*
in the Bekasi region.[19] As early as 2014, Iqbal both spelled out
the preparatory stages for launching a labour party and the
political stances it could take in the meantime. In an opinion
piece in *Koran Perjoeangan* on 31 March 2014,[20] at the time of
the parliamentary and just before the presidential elections,
he wrote:

The first option is that workers' struggle support concepts or
issues of certain parties. There would be a kind of political
contract. In that way the workers' issues would become part of
the agenda that such parties would struggle to achieve.

The second option is to place representatives in several
political parties. This is what the FSPMI and KSPI are doing
at the moment. FSPMI and KSPI cadre are spreading out into
several political parties. We hope that the issues of concern to
workers can be executed by those cadres when they become
members of parliament.

This accurately describes the KSPI/FSPMI policy in relation to the parliamentary and presidential elections. In the same piece, Iqbal affirmed:

> I am of the opinion that such methods can only be temporary. The workers cannot just give their votes to such parties forever. Because of that, establishing a party is a step that must be striven for.

On the next day, in *Koran Perjoeangan*, there appeared another article, "3 Stages That Must be Passed before Establishing a Party".[21] In order to get a sense of a possible time scale for such preparation, it is worth quoting this article in full.

> I am sure we all agree that the workers' party that will one day be formed by the workers must be born out of the needs and wants of the workers themselves. The workers must be asked—in a kind of poll—do they need a political party? In my opinion, a party is inevitable. But the process must involve the workers.
>
> Even so, workers cannot be involved in just any way. Before a union can enter politics, there must be three stages that are passed through: organization, ideologization, and contestation. It is when these three stages are passed through that a political party can be established.
>
> **Organization**
>
> If you have never talked to workers about wages, social insurance, cheap transportation, then suddenly you propose starting a political party to the workers, I am sure that the workers will reject this. They don't see political parties as something they need for their struggles.
>
> Get them involved in the struggle around wages. Involve them in actions that are financed by their own dues. Don't let it happen that the union can be bought. Thus the unions

should have dues. If we start a political party, it should have a dues system. In that way, the party's agenda can't be blocked by others because the workers will be standing on their own feet.

Ideology

After organization is complete, only then we enter into ideologization. At this point the workers are taught about ideology, theories about class from different streams of thought. The awareness of the working class being its own class must be developed.

The trade union must be strong first. If there is no dues payment system, the workers are not organized, then you want to make a party? How would such a party sustain itself? In the end, it would just lead to everything being transactional.

We must make the trade union strong first. It must have a dues system, a program, enough cadre; only then they will say that they need a political party to strengthen their struggle politically.

Contestation

If the organization is good, enough finances, enough cadre, a program and ideology are in effect, only then can we enter contestation. Contestation is the final point, when the ideological and organizational program is completed.

Contestation takes the form of being a political party. This is so the workers can enter the electoral process. It becomes a participant in the elections so that its cadre can be inside the arena for decision making and be a part of deciding the future of the nation.

Its slogan would be, *independent but not neutral.*

It is clear from this article that the launch of a labour party was not seen as looming in the near future. As of July 2017,

although there had been a new initiative—the formation of the
Rumah Rakyat Indonesia as a pre-party mass organization on
May Day 2016—any actual moving closer to this prospect had
not happened. Indeed there was no move to attempt registration
of any new party for the 2019 elections.

Resources are probably not the most significant issue relating
to the prospects of a labour party where the KSPI is a key player.
The most significant is the evident political differences among
the unions now members of or affiliated to Rumah Rakyat. The
two most politically visible components are the KSPI and the
KPBI. The KSPI is, of course, driven by the FSPMI, aligned with
GERINDRA and the PKS; and the KPBI is formed out of unions
that were originally connected to the Sekber Buruh, which was
an initiative of left political groups. The Rumah Rakyat therefore
contains components that are, or appear to be, in serious
contradiction.

Iqbal, in a previously cited statement, explained that orienting
to existing political parties is a necessary interim activity as their
forces prepare the ground for a labour party. Thus it may be the
case that the KSPI's alignment with the GERINDRA-PKS bloc is
purely an interim tactic. And the FSPMI's history of electoral
intervention has been highly opportunistic, the union leadership
having endorsed members to stand with five different parties
as well as one independent candidate. Thus it might be argued
that nothing ideological should be read into these manoeuvres,
and there may not be problems of political differences with the
unions with left origins.

However, the alignment by KSPI/FSPMI with GERINDRA-PKS
in practice has involved the FSPMI/KSPI adopting clear ideological
stances. It involved publicly arguing that human rights are not
a priority concern for workers and that the political history of
General Prabowo in this area was not relevant. During the Jakarta

gubernatorial elections, campaigning by KSPI/FSPMI echoed racist anti-Chinese sentiments. The KSPI/FSPMI also joined the campaign hyping the threat of imported Chinese labour.

The FSPMI/KSPI's decision to fuse their 2016 wage mobilization with the *Bela Islam* mobilization also represents an ideological stance. The mobilization demanded not only the arrest of Governor Purnama but also the ending of the "criminalization of ulama" and the crushing of the Indonesian Communist Party.[22] Anti-communism was also used in 1996 to justify issuing arrest orders for all members of the PRD—from which some of the leaders of the left trade unions in the Rumah Rakyat originate.

The KSPI's own statement, signed by Said Iqbal, included three demands. These were:[23]

1. Repeal government regulation PP 78/2015—reject low wages.
2. Raise the minimum wage by 15–20 per cent.
3. Imprison immediately the accused "Ahok", a demeaner [*sic*] of religion, in the name of the rule of law, as has been the case with others previously accused of this crime.

The statement, which reiterated the KSPI's criticism of Purnama's policies in other areas such as evictions and the Jakarta Bay reclamation, also stated: "The timing of the KSPI's action has been deliberately made to coincide" with the *Bela Islam* action. This is probably the clearest manifestation of the fusion of traditional industrial demands with the ideological stance of the anti-Purnama campaign, accepting the label for Governor Purnama as a "demeaner of religion" and agreeing with the principle that "demeaners of religion" should be imprisoned.

It is significant that the statement was issued by the KSPSI and not by the GBI coalition. There are no examples of the former Sekber Buruh unions in the GBI supporting the anti-Purnama campaign, despite other criticisms they may have had of Purnama's policies. While these unions have not made a point of opposing the KSPI's stand on these ideological issues, neither have they echoed them. This appears to be related to their aim of using the Rumah Rakyat coalition as a step towards a labour party that would include the KSPI. The most active spokespersons for Rumah Rakyat and this trajectory have been activists from the KPBI, former Sekber members of the coalition.

These political differences between two major components of the Rumah Rakyat Indonesia must be a significant challenge to any attempt to form a political party uniting them. A united industrial campaign of unions with different political orientations is already difficult. A political party, usually needing a broader political programme and shared ideological orientation, will clearly be more difficult to achieve, even if not impossible.

As of July 2019, there have been no significant public manifestations of the Rumah Rakyat emerging as an organization heading towards a party.

Notes

1. See Michele Ford, "Learning by Doing: Trade Unions and Electoral Politics in Batam, Indonesia, 2004–2009", *South East Asia Research* 22, no. 3 (2014) 341–57.
2. Ibid.
3. http://nasional.kompas.com/read/2011/05/04/2049576/Kaum.Buruh.Sebaiknya.Bentuk.Parpol.
4. Communication from rank-and-file FSPMI members.
5. She won 255,064 votes, the fourth-highest number of votes of all members of parliament. http://nasional.kompas.com/read/2014/10/01/07150081/Ini.10.Anggota.DPR.2014.dengan.Suara.Terbanyak.di.Indonesia.

6. Amalinda Savarini, "Melawan Oligarki dan Pragmatisme Warga: Gerakan Buruh di Pilkada Kabupaten Bekasi 2017", *Indoprogress*, May 2017, https://indoprogress.com/2017/05/melawan-oligarki-dan-pragmatisme-warga-gerakan-buruh-di-pilkada-kabupaten-bekasi-2017/.

7. The KSPI/FSPMI campaigned for Prabowo Subianto again in the 2019 presidential elections.

8. See the official FSPMI outline of the Sepultura at https://fspmi.or.id/2928.html.

9. http://nasional.kompas.com/read/2014/06/02/1224036/Buruh.KSPI.Deklarasikan.Dukungan.ke.Prabowo-Hatta.

10. http://nasional.kompas.com/read/2014/06/04/0633129/Ini.Sepultura.yang.Prabowo.Janji.Penuhi.

11. "Workers Rally in Jakarta ahead of Wage Negotiations", n.d. http://thejakartaglobe.beritasatu.com/news/jakarta/workers-rally-jakarta-ahead-wage-negotiations/.

12. "Workers Take to the Streets to Protest New Wage Regulation", translated from http://solidaritas.net/2015/11/tuntut-pembatalan-pp-pengupahan-kpr-aksi-di-berbagai-kota.html by APSN's James Balowski.

13. "Labor Union Rejects New Wage Raise Formula", *Jakarta Post*, 16 October 2015, http://www.thejakartapost.com/news/2015/10/16/labor-union-rejects-new-wage-raise-formula.html.

14. "Benarkah Mogok Nasional 2 Desember Mendompleng Aksi Bela Islam III?", http://www.koranperdjoeangan.com/benarkah-mogok-nasional-2-desember-mendompleng-aksi-bela-islam-iii/.

15. http://www.tribunnews.com/metropolitan/2017/04/02/anies-sandi-teken-kontrak-politik-dengan-buruh-ini-janji-mereka.

16. Up until 2019, Governor Baswedan has offered no serious resistance to implementation of this regulation. (For more on the regulation and wages policy, see Appendix 1 to this book.)

17. http://nasional.kompas.com/read/2011/05/04/2049576/Kaum.Buruh.Sebaiknya.Bentuk.Parpol.

18. "Danial Indrakusuma: Serikat Harus Membuat Partai Politik Sendiri"

(interview), https://indoprogress.com/2012/10/danial-indrakusuma-serikat-harus-membuat-partai-politik-sendiri/.

19. Savarini, "Melawan Oligarki dan Pragmatisme Warga".

20. "Said Iqbal, 'Partai Buruh Harus Lahir dari Kepentingan Kaum Buruh, Bukan Elit Pimpinan Buruh'", Koran Perjoeangan.com, http://fspmi.or.id/said-iqbal-partai-buruh-harus-lahir-dari-kepentingan-kaum-buruh-bukan-elit-pimpinan-buruh.html.

21. "Said Iqbal: 3 Tahap yang Harus Dilalui Sebelum Mendirikan Partai", http://fspmi.or.id/said-iqbal-3-tahap-yang-harus-dilalui-sebelum-mendirikan-partai.html.

22. http://politiktoday.com/berhentikan-ahok-hingga-ganyang-pki-tuntutan-aksi-bela-islam-212-jilid-ii-disepakati-dpr/.

23. http://www.kspi.or.id/kspi-resmi-umumkan-mogok-nasional-pada-2-desember-2016.html.

Chapter 5

Conclusions

This essay introduces the politics of the Indonesian trade union movement today, including the crucial factors from before 1998 that have helped create the terrain of today's movement. The essay concentrates on the most visible overt political activities of the most politically active unions. In the preface, I point out that these most active unions represent a minority of union members and an even smaller minority of the workforce, who are mainly not organized into trade unions. However, it would be wrong to imply that workers outside the main unions discussed in this essay are not engaged in industrial activity. Any perusal of the mushrooming number of websites and Facebook groups reporting on industrial activity reveals that there is ongoing workplace disputation. Disputes are happening every week. However, the reporting via these websites and groups provides only a more or less arbitrary coverage of what is happening, depending on the contacts and capacities of the people behind each group or website.

The newness of the labour scene, emphasized in this essay, means that both the mushrooming of workplace unions and sources reporting their activities are fragmented and dispersed. There is no centralized or systematic collection of data or reports.

This also reflects the reality that organized labour itself is still neither centralized nor organized into a unified system. Labour itself is fragmented and dispersed. The fact that a massive proportion of the workforce is employed in enterprises with fewer than twenty employees also means that day-to-day disputes between employees and employers in those enterprises may not take the form of normal union disputes. These smaller enterprises number in the hundreds of thousands.

In these circumstances it is extremely difficult to make any general conclusions about trends in underlying levels of industrial disputation or tensions.

What can be identified are the most explicit manifestations of strongly organized union activity. Even here, the most visible are those activities that insert themselves on to the national political stage. In this essay, the focus has been on the activities initiated by the KSPI/FSPMI and the spectrum of smaller dissident unions. Most observers consider the KSPSI the biggest union, inheriting the majority of the membership of the New Order era single union, but its activities have not significantly inserted the union on to the national political stage. It has been a compliant supporter of the Joko Widodo government and has made only temporary short-term forays into national trade union mobilizations. There are also federations and confederations covering employees of state-owned enterprises. The essay has not sought to focus on them as they too have only made temporary and very short-term forays into national trade union movement mobilizations. There are very many state-owned enterprises, and all are generally unionized. The nature of this unionization from enterprise to enterprise and union to union is also not yet documented nor subject to any intensive or useful analysis.

I restate these points to indicate the nature of the analysis in this short essay. I suspect that any overview of the trade union situation in Indonesia will need to be written with these caveats for some time to come. It may need an escalation in organization, unification and activity before we see the possibility of understanding the whole picture. Again, this is a feature of the newness of the post-1998 labour scene.

Politics of the National Trade Union Movement

The central proposition of the analysis presented here is that, after a period of increased industrial campaigning, the most active trade unions retreated after 2012 and embarked on policies that integrated them into the rivalries of the Indonesian political elite. The basic features of this co-option were the alignment of the most active confederation (KPSI) and federation (FSPMI) with the political party of General Prabowo Subianto, GERINDRA, and its ally the PKS, and the continued alignment of the KSPSI with the PDIP. The alignment of KPSI/FPSMI with GERINDRA and the PKS was the most dramatic in that it constituted a major change in strategy. This change was manifested in the Industrial Harmony Declaration, which framed the demobilization of hitherto escalating industrial militancy. It also involved a turn away from an electoral strategy based on a form of "entryism" into a variety of parties, to an alignment with a specific political bloc. This alignment has not precluded running other campaigns, including supporting union officials running as independents, but it remains a very concrete orientation in a national political scene in which some party rivalries are hardening. It also constitutes a major obstacle to any process of forming a new labour party on the basis of the initial coalitions established to push things in this direction—such as the Rumah Rakyat Indonesia. The alignment with GERINDRA and PKS has brought with it ideological orientations making political unity with the more left-oriented unions difficult and unlikely (although not impossible).

The orientation of KSPI/FSPMI to GERINDRA/PKS and of the KSPSI to the PDIP in effect makes these two major confederations political opponents—at least while GERINDRA consolidates as the major opponent of the Widido-PDIP presidency. At the same time, it situates both the KSPI and KSPSI as having a rival orientation to all of the unions that have emerged directly or indirectly out of the 1990s dissident union and political current. These unions, including the two confederations KASBI and KPBI/SBTPI, as well as the smaller formations such as SEDAR, retain a stance of seeking political representation independently of the existing parties. They have been the most interested in the formation of a new labour party.

Sekber Buruh formed as a coming together of dissident and alternative political blocs. It was Danial Indrakusuma, now associated with solidaritas.net and indirectly with SEDAR, whose advocacy of a labour party was published in the major daily newspaper *Kompas*. The unions in KPBI, including the Federasi Buruh Litans Pabrik and the SBTPI, entered into alliances during 2014–17 with the KSPI/FBSI, openly advocating that they combine to form a new party, and jointly launched the Rumah Rakyat Indonesia, which has since seemingly stalled. SEDAR, a much smaller formation, and activists such as Indrakusuma are pushing forward a multi-sectoral alliance, the Persatuan Perjuangan Rakyat Indonesia (PPRI—Indonesian People's Struggle Front), which could be assessed as the potential core of a political bloc in which labour also played a role. For the moment, the KPBI and PPRI are separate formations divided by disagreement over how to orient to the KSPI/FSPMI (and perhaps other issues), but this whole process is still at a very early stage. Also, the SBSI and the KSN (aligned to the PRP) have been rumoured to be in negotiations

about working through the Partai Buruh, established originally
by Muchtar Pakpahan.

In summary, there are for now two significant politically
active labour blocs—each internally divided. One is the KSPSI and
KSPI bloc defined by the orientation to existing political parties,
although they orient to parties currently opposed to each other.
The other is the KPBI, SEDAR/PPRI, SBSI and KSN bloc, which still
advocates the formation of a new political party independent of
the major existing parties. Into this second bloc, we may need to
place KASBI, which appears to reject alignments with the existing
parties but has not been part of any of the processes aimed at
forming a new party.

Assessment of Potential Trajectories

The history and sociology of the Indonesian working class do not
provide a likely basis for the emergence of the social democratic
style trade union movement that played a significant role in the
emergence of a welfare state in Europe, Australia, New Zealand,
Canada and to a certain extent the United States. As in most of the
formerly colonized world, low levels of general industrialization
are creating a working class made up of a huge majority of
informal or semi-proletarians working in small enterprises or in
an "informal sector" of peddlers and handymen, a small minority
in more formal employment, and an even smaller minority in
medium or large enterprises. This means that only a very small
minority of workers are ever organized into serious unions,
although these are often in the most strategic sectors where the
most "value-added" is produced.

In Indonesia, this situation is made more complicated—made
worse from the point of view of forming strong unions—by the
very long period of state authoritarian unionism, which has left

the working class without any experience or tradition of unionism or labour politics. The organizable small minority in medium and large enterprises enter the union world inexperienced and with no reference points. They also encounter a union world characterized by a myriad of newly formed unions, federations and confederations—that is to say very organizationally divided. This makes difficult and even unlikely the emergence of a strong labour movement, built upon trade unions, that can champion a welfare state—at least in terms of the model recognized in the advanced capitalist countries. That model has not been replicated in any undeveloped, unindustrialized countries.

Beyond Unionized Workers

The sociological profile outlined above immediately gives rise to the conclusion that popular discontent with low incomes and poor material conditions cannot be confined to being based on unionized workers alone. They are too small a proportion of the working population and too organizationally divided and inexperienced. This idea is increasingly recognized among the actors in the union sector.

The decision of the KSPI and KPBI to form the Rumah Rakyat Indonesia, although now stalled, was based on the idea that organized workers needed to reach beyond their own ranks to the (semi-proletariat) urban poor as well as farmers. The choice of the word *rakyat* (the common people) rather than *buruh* (worker) was a deliberate decision related to this idea. Similarly, the PPRI is a multi-sectoral grouping aiming to organize beyond unionized workers.

Unionized workers were a small minority, divided and weak, although they displayed their potential to be a strong, organized spearhead force during the 2010–12 period. The realization of that potential requires not only overcoming the existing divisions and experiential weakness, but also the discovery of strategy and tactics that can reach out and lead forces beyond themselves. Attempts to form multi-sectoral groupings like Rumah Rakyat or PPRI, whatever their immediate fate, are a reflection of the awareness of this necessity. However, once this prospect is contemplated, the "ideological" basis for organizing, mobilizing and agitating a much broader social coalition than the unionized workers of medium and large enterprises becomes an issue. In this context, the phenomenon called "populism"—an agitational appeal to a broad coalition of the various segments of the poor and popular classes against the elite or against groups identified as the cause of popular poverty and economic backwardness— becomes relevant. This has become an increasingly evident feature of contemporary Indonesian politics, and of political contestation within organized labour. It is reflected in the KSPI/FSPMI's and other unions' alliance with the Islamic populism initially targeted against Governor Purnama and President Widodo. That populism alleges that Chinese, infidels, communists and false Muslims are the cause of the suffering of the popular classes—redefined as the *ummah*. This is not the place to discuss in depth the populism of President Widodo, which is not agitational but rather aimed at the pacification of discontent. All the same, his positioning of himself close to the "little people", even to the extent of explicitly reminding people of his "village face", while blaming bureaucracy and over-regulation for the suffering of the "little people", is also a form of populism. For the moment, the KSPSI as a supporter of President Widodo is aligned with this populism.

The bloc still oriented to forming an independent labour party—the KPBI and PPRI/SEDAR—will also inevitably be drawn into a contestation over which form of populism will win majority support among any potential broad alignment of social sectors. The contours of possible programmes and strategies that may emerge from this bloc are not yet clear. The KPBI's attempt to ally with the KSPI/FSPMI in the formation of Rumah Rakyat Indonesia and its apparent failure have without doubt delayed an independent approach in relation to this challenge. The PPRI, with a very small union base, is still at too early a stage of activity for its programme and strategy to be clear. Neither grouping has any substantial policy or strategy documents.

Unpredictability

Unions like KPSI/FNPBI, KSPSI, KPBI and SEDAR as they have evolved over the last ten years will most likely continue to be major players in the further development of the labour movement, and in any broader social or political movements that may evolve. In concluding, however, it is necessary to return to the point made at the beginning of this essay and in the opening paragraphs of this conclusion: these unions represent both a minority of the formal workforce and an even smaller minority of the total workforce. At the same time, the ongoing industrial disputation reported in the social and labour media and the various sympathetic responses to different forms of populist politics indicate that the big majority of the working population outside of the unions cannot be considered to be permanent non-players in future contestations, including in the short term.

Any ongoing assessment of the trends identified in this essay must remain sensitive to the potential for unpredictable developments. To bring this introductory essay up to date, two 2018 commentary pieces on labour politics have been added as appendices.

Epilogue

On 17 April 2019, Indonesia held presidential and parliamentary elections. It would appear from the most recent results from the General Election Commission (80 per cent counted) that the incumbent President Joko Widodo has won the elections with approximately 55–56 per cent of the vote—although the other candidate, Prabowo Subianto, claims that there was extensive cheating and that he won the election. During the election campaign, trade union alignments did not vary significantly from what has been described in this essay. The KSPSI and KSBSI supported President Widodo. The KPSI, including the FSPMI, supported Prabowo Subianto. Prabowo Subianto included Said Iqbal on the list of prospective ministers.[1] The trade unions emerging from anti-elite dissident streams refused to support either candidate or advocated abstaining from voting—known in Indonesia as the GOLPUT position. This was the position of KASBI, KPBI and the federation F-SEDAR.[2] GOLPUT was supported by almost all of the groups that participated in the April 2018 Konperensi Gerakan Rakyat Indonesia (KGRI—Indonesian Peoples Movement Conference). For more on the KGRI, see Appendix 2 in this volume.

During the election campaign, some of those groups advocating GOLPUT also advocated that groups that rejected both the Widodo and Subianto camps should start moving towards forming a political bloc or organization of their own in order to present an alternative. This is also consistent with the resolutions of the KGRI. While almost all the trade unions that advocated GOLPUT are now also discussing the possibility or supporting the idea of forming an alternative political bloc, they have not formed a single coalition working towards this aim. Two weeks after the elections, when May Day mobilizations took place, those unions not aligned to Widodo or Subianto mobilized through the two coalitions that emerged during 2018, GEBRAK (whose core forces are KASBI and KPBI) and KOMITMEN (whose core forces are F-SEDAR and a spectrum of smaller unions and activist groups). (On the emergence of GEBRAK and KOMITMEN, see Appendix 2 in this volume.) On 1 May[3] the GEBRAK mobilization was reported as being the larger of the two that took place that day, but both mobilizations are being viewed as serious and dynamic. (There are reports that elements from within KASBI mobilized separately.) The existence of these two coalitions among trade unions indicates that there are still issues differentiating them. In addition, during the election campaign there were other groups advocating for the need for a new political alternative, which also included unions, though smaller. These included a coalition that included PRP and PPI.

In May 2019 it is still too soon to attempt a description and analysis of the issues differentiating these groups. These issues may be better analysed after the electoral outcome is confirmed and the policy contours of the government become clearer. It is then that the contours of any union-based opposition to the new government would also become clearer.

In the immediate aftermath of the elections, and prior to May Day, President Widodo repeated the gesture he had previously made before May Day of inviting trade union leaders to meet him in the Presidential Palace. All the leaders of the main confederations attended, except KASBI. At the time of writing, it is not clear why a KASBI leader did not attend. Soon after the meeting, some union activists—tanker drivers who had been detained after a union action on charges related to their use of the tankers—were released. The national police also announced that they had set up a desk to deal with complaints from workers against employers alleged to have broken industrial laws. There have also been commitments during the campaign by both Widodo and Subianto to review regulations impacting on wages policy (see Appendix 1).

Notes

1. https://nasional.kompas.com/read/2019/03/28/19120291/saat-prabowo-perkenalkan-para-calon-menteri-dari-ahy-hingga-said-iqbal.
2. For KPBI's position, see http://www.mediakajianstrategis indonesiaglobal.com/2019/01/29/sikap-politik-kelas-buruh-dalam-menghadapi-pemilu-2019/; for KASBI's position, see, for example, https://tirto.id/membedah-potensi-gelombang-golput-di-pilpres-2019-cRYi; for Federasi SEDAR, see https://fsedar.org/kabar/gelar-pemungutan-suara-805-anggota-fsedar-pilih-golput/.
3. See https://nasional.kompas.com/read/2018/04/27/17281341/may-day-2018-buruh-akan-serukan-pembentukan-politik-alternatif; for KOMITMEN, see https://www.facebook.com/permalink.php?id=381652612341872&story_fbid=571696806670784; also, https://korankejora.blogspot.com/2019/04/pernyataan-sikap-komitmen-komite-1-mei.html?m=1.

Max Lane

13 May 2019

Appendix 1:
The Politics of Wages and Indonesia's Trade Unions

On 1 April 2017, thirteen trade unions, having formed a coalition, signed a "Political Contract" with two candidates in the Jakarta gubernatorial elections.[1] These thirteen unions then gave their support to Anies Baswedan and Sandiaga Uno, candidates nominated by the Partai Keadilan Sejahtera (PKS) and GERINDRA, the party headed by the 2014 presidential candidate, Prabowo Subianto. These unions included the Konfederasi Serikat Pekerja Indonesia (KSPI), Federasi Serikat Pekerja Metal Indonesia (FSPMI), and Serikat Pekerja Nasional (SPN),[2] among others. The KSPI and FSPMI leaderships had been supporting the GERINDRA-PKS coalition since the 2014 presidential elections. Between 2010 and 2013, the KSPI and FPSMI had been the vanguard of a series of annual campaigns for increases in the minimum wage and ending the widespread use of labour hire (called "outsourcing").

The points included in the Political Contract covered wages, labour hire, housing, public transport, unemployment social

Originally published as *ISEAS Perspective*, no. 4/2018 (18 January 2018).

insurance, education, the Jakarta Bay reclamation,[3] the status of teachers, health insurance and workers cooperatives. The one point made on wages policy was as follows:

> To decide the Jakarta DKI minimum wage higher than that determined by Government Regulation No 78 2015 about Wages, through the Wage Council mechanism, and to set sectoral wage scale and structure based on Law 13 2003 on Labour.[4]

Anies Baswedan and Sandiaga Una won the elections—for many reasons beyond the wages issue—and were sworn in as governor and vice-governor on 16 October 2017. Two weeks later, on 1 November, the new governor signed-off on the minimum wage for 2018. He did not conform to the wages policy point in the Political Contract but determined a wage increase based on Regulation 78/2015, not higher. The new minimum wage was determined as Rp3,648,035, an 8.7 per cent increase on the previous year. The unions were asking for Rp3,917,398.[5]

As a consequence of this decision, the thirteen unions held a press conference and declared that they were withdrawing their support for Anies Baswedan. The president of the KSPI and FSPMI, Said Iqbal, even compared Baswedan unfavourably with former governor and now prisoner Basuki Basuki Tjahaja Purnama, saying that the latter was a more honourable man than Baswedan.[6] During the gubernatorial campaign, Iqbal had been very critical of Purnama on a range of issues,[7] and had merged his unions with major protests that were calling for Purnama to be arrested for humiliating Islam.[8] Iqbal had also been critical of Purnama's policy on wages, criticizing the fact that wages in Jakarta under Purnama were lower than those in Karawang District, outside Jakarta. However, after the Baswedan decision, Iqbal acknowledged that Purnama himself, in 2016, had determined a wage increase *above* that based on Regulation 78/2015. Purnama did comply with Regulation 78/2015 in determining the minimum wage for 2017.

Wage Regulations in Indonesia

The primary aspect of wages regulated in Indonesia is the level of the minimum wage. Law No. 13 of 2003 on Labour legislated that the government, at national and local levels, would set a minimum wage. This minimum wage was to be "based on [an assessment of] dignified living needs and paying attention to productivity and economic growth (*berdasarkan kebutuhan hidup layak dan dengan memperhatikan produktivitas dan pertumbuhan ekonomi*).[9]

Between 2003 and 2014, the assessment of the minimum wage occurred annually. Usually the review began in October–November and the results for the year were announced in December or on 1 January.

The law also established a Wages Council at the national, provincial and district/city level.[10] A minimum wage was to be set for each province, and the productivity of each economic sector in each province was to be assessed. The membership of the council was appointed by the president, governor, *bupati* or mayor, depending on the level. The membership comprised two representatives of the Ministry of Labour (who would act as chair and secretary), one representative of a trade union and one of an employers' association. These councils could also appoint expert members.[11]

These councils would make recommendations to the local government head, such as the governor, *bupati* or mayor. The local government heads would make the final decision. Their position was, and still is, central. However, governors usually accepted recommendations coming from the *bupati* or mayor, making these officials also crucial.

Since 2003, these committees would receive inputs from trade unions, employers' associations and the government as to what was an acceptable Kebutuhan Hidup Layak (KHL—Dignified Living Needs). Assessments of productivity and economic growth were usually based on official statistics, with productivity reportedly also sometimes disputed. The main focus of disputation was the KHL. Trade unions and employers' groups often had very different assessments, often reflected in different baskets of goods used to assess the cost of living and the quality of product deemed necessary. Crucial also was the unions' assertion that wages had been neglected for a long-time and had been under the KHL, and therefore needed large catch-up increases.

Over the seven-year period between 2004 and 2010, after the new legislation was passed, the official minimum wage for Jakarta increased from Rp671,000 to Rp1,118,009. Wages increased even further during the shorter period 2011–14, especially in areas where factory workers were concentrated. The main factory belt near Jakarta is spread through the districts of Bekasi, Tangerang and Karawang.

The Politics of Wage Campaigning: 2010–13

During 2010, a new coalition of trade unions, non-government organizations and a few activist members of parliament ran a successful campaign, combining large union-based protest mobilizations, litigation and lobbying to pressure parliament to pass legislation to advance the implementation of social insurance, especially for health. This campaign came after approximately ten years of consolidation of a spectrum of new union formations.

The success of the campaign boosted confidence among some unions in public industrial campaigning. The campaign focussed on demands for substantial wage increases and the suppression of illegal labour hire practices known as "outsourcing".

Various different combinations of unions participated in the campaigns each year. However, the Indonesian Trade Union Confederation (KSPI—Konfederasi Serikat Pekerja Indonesia), which contained the very well organized Federation of Indonesian Metal Unions (FSPMI—Federasi Serikat Pekerja Metal Indonesia), was the leading force in these mobilizations.

Between 2011 and 2013, these campaigns achieved some substantial wage increases, but little in reducing "outsourcing". This period was also the lead-up to parliamentary elections, including in electorates within the factory belt area on the edge of Jakarta. Given the crucial role of the *bupati* in wage determination for their districts, they came under heavy pressure in the face of a combination of large-scale campaigning—protests, demonstrations, strikes—and electoral campaigning. One of the most popular politicians in the region, Rieke Diah Pitaloka, a member of parliament in one of the affected electorates, was a supporter of the union campaigns. The issue was high on the agenda of electoral politics, even if, in the end, it was not the only major issue.

The campaigns were large scale and began with assemblies of tens of thousands of workers on May Day in Senayan, Jakarta's biggest sports stadium. There were warm up actions between May and October, mostly involving mobilizations, and also actions to close down major highways. The largest mobilizations, with some strikes, would take place in October–November.

The largest increase was that announced at the end of 2012 for 2013. The year 2013 would be the one before parliamentary and then presidential elections. In Karawang, the minimum wage went from Rp1,269,227 to Rp2,102,000 and then up to Rp2,447,450 for 2014.[12] The increases in other nearby factory belt electorates were similar. By 2014, the minimum wage in Jakarta had risen to Rp2,441,000 from Rp1,118,009 in 2010.[13] In 2013, Joko Widodo became Governor of Jakarta and was already looking towards standing for president in 2014.

Campaign De-escalation: Prelude to New Wage Regulation

The period of intense industrial campaigning ended with the signing of the Bekasi Industrial Harmony Declaration on 8 November 2013.[14] The declaration contained six points. Although they were all formulated in very general terminology, it was clearly a declaration against conflict and militancy. The final points emphasized the need to create a climate in which enterprises could be productive and develop in a competitive environment. The emphasis was on consensus, cooperation and developing industrial relations in which all benefited. Representatives of the unions were Obon Tabroni, president of the Bekasi branch of the FSPMI; R. Abdullah, Bekasi head of the KSPSI; Joko Tugimin, Bekasi president of the Serikat Pekerja Nasional (SPN—National Workers' Union); and Sepriyanto, Bekasi head of the Gabungan Serikat Pekerja Manufaktur Independen Indonesia (GSPMII—Indonesian Independent Manufacturing Trade Unions Combination).

Employer representatives were Sutopo, head of the Bekasi branch of the Indonesian Employers Association (Apindo–Asosiasi Pengusaha Indonesia); Dedi Wijaja, head of the West Java Apindo; Obing Fachruddin, head of the Bekasi Chamber of

Commerce and Industry (Kadin); Sanny Iskandar, Bekasi head of the Himpunan Kawasan Industri Kabupaten Bekasi; and Deddy Harsono, chairperson of the Forum Investor Bekasi.

The declaration was also signed by the governor of West Java, Ahmad Heryawan, and the *bupati* of Bekasi, Neneng Hasanah Yasin, as well as by village heads, members of parliament and an Islamic community figure. Two military officers with the rank of colonel heading up local army commands also signed, as did the head of the Bekasi police.

This declaration at the end of 2013 occurred during the same period that the president of the KPSI and FSPMI declared his support for the candidacy of Prabowo Subianto for the Indonesian presidency. The FSPMI stood candidates in the 2014 parliamentary elections in local seats under the banners of several different parties. The open declaration of support for Subianto went beyond this approach, aligning the KPSI and FSPMI with Subianto and with the parties supporting Subianto, primarily GERINDRA and the Islamist-oriented Party of Justice and Welfare (PKS—Partai Keadilan Sejahtera). Iqbal himself had stood as a PKS candidate in the 2009 parliamentary elections.

As the leading union formation of 2010–13 de-escalated industrial campaigning in accord with the 2013 declaration, and saw a clear alignment with one political bloc, the political terrain of labour relations altered dramatically. The other large union confederation, the All Indonesia Confederation of Trade Unions (KSPSI—Konfederasi Serikat Pekerja Seluruh Indonesia),[15] supported the Joko Widodo presidency. The two biggest unions were each aligned with one of the two major political blocs. KSPSI had been a part of the coalition that had joined the industrial campaigning coalition in its early phase, but by 2012–13 it was no longer a serious participant.

New Wage Regulation:
Presidential Regulation 78/2015

Industrial campaigning around the minimum wage during 2014
and 2015 was considerably weaker than in previous years. The year
2014 was also dominated by the parliamentary and presidential
elections, where the major union confederations had aligned
themselves. There was another round of wage increases set at the
end of 2014 for 2015. However, in October 2015 the government
issued a new regulation that substantially changed the system
for setting the minimum wage. This change was opposed, and
is still opposed—at least formally—by all the unions,[16] but to
no effect. With industrial campaigning de-escalated and being
aligned to political blocs who either supported or accepted the
new regulation, the unions became ineffective.

The new regulation was PERATURAN PEMERINTAH REPUBLIK
INDONESIA, NOMOR 78 TAHUN 2015 TENTANG PENGUPAHAN,
referred to as regulation 78/2015. This regulation ended the
annual review of the minimum wage and replaced it with a
combination of automatic annual increases based on an official
formula, and five-yearly reviews of wages by the Wages Council,
as currently composed. The formula that was designated to set
the minimum wage removed the Dignified Living Needs (KHL)
calculation from wage setting, using only the official statistics for
productivity and economic growth. Wages would be increased
by a percentage equivalent to productivity and economic growth
added together.

The Political Contract between the Jakarta Union Coalition and
Anies Baswedan during the 2017 Jakarta gubernatorial campaign
agreed to an increase beyond the new formula, implying that it
would take into account to some extent the KHL, as mandated
by the 2003 legislation. There were no exact figures agreed to.

Wages, Unions and Politics

The decision by Governor Baswedan to set the wage increase at 8.7 per cent was met with criticism and protest from the KSPI and FSMPI, articulated by union president Said Iqbal. Baswedan and his deputy, Sandiaga Una, are from the political bloc that the KSPI has aligned with since 2014.[17] The question arises then as to whether this difference over wage policy is undermining the KSPI/FSPMI's alignment with that bloc. This question may only be answered definitely in the coming period and into the 2019 elections. However, it can be noted that the FSPMI newspaper *Koran Perjoeangan* published an article entitled "Exposed. So This is What Frightened the Governors Who Then Persisted in Implementing PP 78/2015" ("Terbongkar. Ternyata Ini Yang Ditakutkan Gubernur Sehingga Ngotot Terapkan PP 78/2015").[18] This article refers to an official letter sent by the Minister of Home Affairs on 30 October 2017 to all governors reminding them that they were obliged to conform with and implement national policy and national government regulations.[19] The letter from the minister sets out a series of sanctions for non-compliance, beginning with written warnings, through suspension and then dismissal. The letter makes no mention of Regulation 78/2015 or any other specific regulation. With this article, *Koran Perjoeangan* shifts at least some of the blame back on to the national government of President Widodo. This is possibly an indication that the FSPMI will retain its current alignment.

Meanwhile, the other large leading union, the KSPSI, appears to remain aligned with President Widodo, although some regional branches are still condemning Regulation 78/2015.

It is likely that given the political alignments and industrial campaigning tactics that have evolved since 2013, there is little immediate threat to the continuation of the government's new wage policy as manifested in Regulation 78/2015. It is less clear what the medium-term impact will be on union politics. The KSPSI and KSPI are not the only union confederations in Indonesia, and there are also federations and individual workplace unions that are not aligned to either of the two major electoral political blocs operating at national level politics. One growing confederation is the Confederation of Indonesian Trade Unions Alliances Congress[20] (KASBI—Konfederasi Kongres Aliansi Serikat Buruh Indonesia), which has been campaigning for a 31 per cent increase in the minimum wage across the board.[21] KASBI claims to represent around 130,000 members. Another new confederation, the Indonesian Workers United Confederation (KPBI—Kongres Persatuan Buruh Indonesia),[22] which includes port-based drivers and others, is also unaligned to a political bloc and continues to raise concerns around the KHL. Individual federations such as the newly formed Popular Democratic Union Federation[23] (Sedar—Federasi Serikat Demokratik Kerakyatan) have also organized successful campaigns in individual workplaces. KASBI, KPBI and Federasi Sedar are just a few examples of the many confederations, federations and individual unions that have emerged and are still emerging in Indonesia since the end of the New Order and which have not aligned with any political bloc. There are many others.[24] If the alignments of the bigger unions continue to restrict their room to manoeuvre and campaign, there will be increased space for other unions to grow.

Notes

1. https://news.detik.com/berita/d-3462402/13-organisasi-buruh-jakarta-dukung-anies-sandiaga; https://www.merdeka.com/peristiwa/anies-sandi-teken-kontrak-politik-dengan-koalisi-buruh-jakarta.html.
2. http://nasional.republika.co.id/berita/nasional/politik/17/04/01/onq2fk384-buruh-sejakarta-deklarasi-dukung-aniessandi.

3. The Jakarta Bay Reclamation issue was used by the opposition to Governor Purnama and adopted by these unions.
4. http://jakarta.bisnis.com/read/20171110/77/707977/10-kontrak-politik-buruh-jakarta-dengan-anies-sandi.
5. http://megapolitan.kompas.com/read/2017/11/02/09323181/penetapan-ump-dki-2018-dan-asas-keadilan-menurut-anies-sandi.
6. http://megapolitan.kompas.com/read/2017/11/02/18545951/said-iqbal-ternyata-ahok-jauh-lebih-ksatria-ketimbang-anies-sandi.
7. https://www.koranperdjoeangan.com/sinetron-hukum-gubernur-ahok/; https://www.koranperdjoeangan.com/10-kegagalan-gubernur-ahok-memimpin-jakarta/.
8. https://www.koranperdjoeangan.com/mogok-nasional-2-desember-buruh-bantah-dompleng-umat-islam/.
9. Section 88, clause 4: UNDANG-UNDANG REPUBLIK INDONESIA NOMOR 13 TAHUN 2003 TENTANG KETENAGAKERJAAN.
10. Ibid., section 98.
11. The details of these Wages Councils are set out in the following presidential decision: KEPUTUSAN PRESIDEN REPUBLIK INDONESIA NOMOR 107 TAHUN 2004 TENTANG DEWAN PENGUPAHAN.
12. See http://regional.kompas.com/read/2013/11/22/0323461/Ini.Upah.Minimum.di.Kabupaten.Kota.Jawa.Barat. See also "Keputusan Gubernur Jawa Barat, Nomor: 561/Kep.1540.Bangsos/2011 Tentang Upah Minimum Kabupaten/Kota Di Jawa Barat Tahun 2012", https://mantanburuh.files.wordpress.com/2011/12/sk_umk-jabar_tahun_2012.pdf.
13. For minimum wages across the country between 1997 and 2016, see official statistics at https://www.bps.go.id/linkTableDinamis/view/id/917.
14. *Kompas*, 8 November 2012, http://megapolitan.kompas.com/read/2012/11/08/17052399/Deklarasi.Harmoni.Industri.Bekasi.Didukung.
15. The KSPSI was not party to the Political Contract with Anies Baswedan and Sandiaga Una. Central members of its leadership have been close to the PDIP.

16. This includes the unions, such as KSPSI and KSBSI, that supported Joko Widodo in the 2014 elections.

17. Interestingly, in local elections in 2014 the FSPMI did field one candidate as an independent. It is not clear yet whether this represented significant experimentation with a non-aligned strategy.

18. "Terbongkar. Ternyata Ini Yang Ditakutkan Gubernur Sehingga Ngotot Terapkan PP 78/2015", *Koran Perjoeangan*, 4 December 2017, https://www.koranperdjoeangan.com/terbongkar-ternyata-ini-yang-ditakutkan-gubernur-sehingga-ngotot-terapkan-pp-782015/.

19. The article refers to "Surat Edaran Menteri Dalam Negeri Republik Indonesia Nomor 561/7721/SJ".

20. See the KASBI website at https://kasbi.or.id/.

21. https://news.detik.com/berita/d-3706167/tuntutan-massa-buruh-kenaikan-upah-hingga-hapus-outsourcing?utm_medium=oa&utm_campaign=detikcomsocmed&utm_source=facebook&utm_content=detikcom.

22. See buruh.co/tentang-kpbi for the KPBI website.

23. See fsedar.org.

24. There are probably also smaller unions aligned with parties in the two big national electoral blocs, through connections to individual parties—although they do not yet have any significant national profile.

Appendix 2:
Trade Unions' Initiative to Create Alternative Political Force in Indonesia

During the first months of 2018, the prospect of non-aligned unions using the space left open to them as the larger union confederations consolidated their alignments with the two major electoral blocs looked like it might be realized quicker than expected. KASBI (Kongres Aliansi Serikat Buruh Indonesia; Indonesian Trade Union Congress Alliance Confederation), KPBI (Konfederasi Persatuan Buruh Indonesia, Confederation of United Indonesian Workers), Federasi Sedar (Serikat Buruh Demokratik Kerakyatan; Populist Democratic Trade Union) and two other non-aligned federations agreed to host a joint political conference to which other non-aligned unions, as well as non-government organizations and political groups would be invited.[1] The conference took place in April 2018, shortly before the annual May Day trade union mobilizations.

Originally published as *ISEAS Perspective*, no. 44/2018 (10 August 2018).

Before analysing the conference and its immediate aftermath, including its apparent stall, it is useful to look at some of the immediate context beyond the trends discussed in an earlier *ISEAS Perspective.*[2]

There appeared to be two trends developing into 2018 that helped push the union leaderships in this direction. Neither of these were new trends, but they evolved to a higher level, impacting on the thinking of the unions.

First, the best resourced and organized and, until 2013, the most activist confederation, the KSPI (Konfederasi Serikat Pekerja Indonesia; Confederation of Indonesian Trade Unions), with the FSPMI (Federasi Serikat Pekerja Metal Indonesia; Indonesian Metal Trade Workers Federation) as its vanguard, further deepened its alignment with the 2019 presidential candidacy of Prabowo Subianto. KSPI/FSPMI had openly supported Prabowo in 2014 and had maintained the relationship since then, despite one of its leaders also standing as an independent candidate in a district election in 2017. In late 2017 and into early 2018, rumours began to spread that KSPI/FSPMI, still under the leadership of chairperson Said Iqbal, would again announce its support for Prabowo at its rally on May Day. By March, there were news reports of Iqbal's still positive assessment of Prabowo.[3]

At the same time, rumours strengthened that the other major union confederation, the KSPSI (Konfederasi Serikat Pekerja Seluruh Indonesia; Confederation of the All-Indonesian Workers Union) under the leadership of Yorrys Raweyai would announce support for President Joko Widodo also on 1 May, May Day.

It was being confirmed that the process of the two major confederations consolidating their alignment with either Widodo or Prabowo was going to be the reality for 2019. Indeed, both the confederations did make these announcements on 1 May.[4]

Even as early as January, some of the leaders of the non-aligned unions had begun to think about how to respond.

There was also a second trend challenging these non-aligned union leaders, many of whom had been part of the moderately left-oriented movement that was in opposition to the Suharto government before 1998. This was the challenge, probably best thought of as occurring at the ideological level, of the agitation aimed at the memberships from the increasingly activist conservative Islamist organizations. Union organizers report that such Islamist organizations were increasingly reaching out to union members. The strength of the trade unions is in the factory belts on the edge of Jakarta, in Tangerang, Bekasi and Karawang. This area of West Java, like the province as a whole, is an area where conservative Islam has always been strong. Ethnically Sundanese (and not Javanese), this area has seen Islamic culture evolve without the influence of syncretic Javanism. The political party MASYUMI and the armed Islamist rebellion of Darul Islam had both been strong in this region since the 1950s. In the current period, it is also an area where organizations such as the FPI (Front Pembela Islam; Islamic Defenders Front) and similar organizations are active. There have even been rallies in West Java in support of ISIS and against the arrests of ISIS supporters.

As has been noted in debates in the publication *New Mandala*, the entry point of these organizations into the poorer kampongs of outer Jakarta, where factory workers also live, was often over socio-economic grievances.[5] Reflecting these trends, conservative Islamism, said some union organizers, was becoming an ideology competing with the progressive sentiments being cultivated within the unions. Conservative political Islamism offered what was presented as a holistic solution to the plight of the urban poor, usually in the form of one variant or another of a more religiously organized polity. This ranged from a polity where Islamic law (*syariah*) and Islamic leadership authority (*kyai* and ulama) would be given a more influential role through to the full Islamic caliphate advocated by the Hizbut Tahrir Indonesia (HTI). The HTI's policy on trade unions was that under such a caliphate they should be abolished.

These Islamist forces were also either aligning with the Prabowo political bloc, manifested in the core alliance between GERINDRA (Partai Gerakan Indonesia Raja; Great Indonesia Movement Party) and PKS (Partai Keadilan Sejahtera; Justice and Prosperity Party), or at least making clear their hostility to the Widodo alliance.

Among union leaderships there arose a discussion that the non-aligned progressive unions needed to respond to these political and ideological challenges. Five confederations or federations, after discussion, issued a joint invitation for other unions, non-government organizations and political groups to attend a Konperensi Gerakan Rakyat (KGR—Peoples Movement Congress) on 19–20 April.[6]

Peoples Movement Congress—KGR

The five unions issuing the invitation for the congress were the Indonesian Trade Union Congress Alliance (KASBI), the Confederation of United Indonesian Workers (KPBI), the Popular Democratic Trade Union (SEDAR), the KSN (Konfederasi Serikat Nasional; National Union Confederation), and the SGBN (Sentral Gerakan Buruh Nasional; National Labour Movement Centre). In the invitation, attending the congress was described as a chance to exchange ideas about the best ways to respond to contemporary developments. To help create a conducive attitude for such a gathering, a trial joint mobilization was organized for International Women's Day in March.[7] The five unions also issued a joint statement with fourteen demands. The statement not only included demands for an end to discrimination against women, for menstrual leave and for equal pay, it also provided a general critique of what was described as neo-liberal social and economic policies and a series of demands for general social and economic reform.[8] The mobilization was a modest but symbolically significant action in the lead up to the KGR.

The conference was attended by at least forty-three organizations, all of which signed a joint declaration.[9] Some participants said that at various times during the conference there were up to seventy organizations represented.[10] There were reported to be at least six hundred people attending.[11] The forty-three organizations were made up of seven trade union groupings and a trade union support centre; seven university student organizations; three urban poor organizations: one Christian and two progressive Islamic organizations; two farmers' organizations; a major environmental organization; a Papuan students' organization; two women's rights organizations; five human rights organizations; a cultural activist organization and six left-wing political groups.[12]

The declared theme of the conference was Freedom, Equality and Prosperity.

There were two major outcomes of the conference. The first was the confirmation that a broad sentiment exists for the formation of a political alternative to the existing political parties, although there were differences expressed on what the basis for forming such an alternative should be. The second outcome was a declaration agreed to by forty-three of the organizations present. The declaration contains a statement of mandate and a list of policy demands.[13] The first of these declares that the Mandate of the Indonesian People's Movement Conference is:

- To recommend to the individual organisations involved in the conference to discuss building an alternative political force.
- To establish a team to discuss the formation of an alternative political force (an alternative political party or alternative political block).
- To hold follow-up consolidations [sic] with the broader people's movement to discuss building an alternative political force in July this year.

It lists the urgent demands of the people as follows:

- Develop a national industry under the control of the people.
- Nationalise strategic assets such as state-owned enterprises, mining and infrastructure.
- Genuine agrarian reform.
- Increase subsidies for the people in education, healthcare, housing and transportation.
- Revoke the laws on elections and political parties.
- Abolish the military's territorial command structure.
- Abolish anti-democratic legislation (the Perppu Ormas, UU MD3 and the UU ITE).
- Try and jail corruptors and seize their assets.
- Address the welfare and human rights violations in Papua and respect the Papuan people's right to struggle for self-determination.
- Protect women's rights (maternity leave, breastfeeding and an end to sexual violence) and end discrimination based on sexual orientation, race or religion.
- Free, scientific and democratic education.
- A decent national minimum wage and the revocation of Government Regulation 78/2015 on Wages.

- Abolish contract labour systems and outsourcing and enact legislation on the protection of workers.
- Fully investigate and resolve past human rights violations.
- Universal social welfare, not social insurance.
- Protection for migrant workers prior to and after placement.
- An end to the exploitation of natural resources and the destruction of the environment.
- Stop the forced eviction of the poor from their land.

It is important to be able to read all these demands so that the nature of the conference is clear. First, we can note that the demands are not at all simply confined to demands normally connected to concerns of unions such as wages and working conditions. Reflecting the sentiments in the mandate, these demands are more reflective of the range of policy demands a political movement or party might make than the narrower spectrum of traditional trade union demands. Second, we can also note that the demands are formulated in general terms, without any specific detail. This underlined the fact that this was an initial, experimental conference that, in the eyes of key participants, was not yet a decision-making conference, but a forum for the exchange of ideas.

Difficulties for Unification

The call for an "alternative political force" immediately raises the challenge of unification among these groups. An "alternative force" implies either an organized political movement or a party. Among the many union members, there were reported differences on whether moving in this direction should be done quickly or slowly.[14] There were also echoes of the long-standing difference among the five union sponsors over the question of how to orientate towards the KSPI/FSPMI. One confederation, the KPBI, has been participating in various alliances, albeit loose ones, with the KSPI/FSMPI. The KPBI has also supported the formation of the Rumah Rakyat Indonesia (House of the Indonesian People)[15] as an attempt at a pre-party formation. Some participants reported that KPBI participants who spoke still held out this hope.[16] Other unions, such as KASBI and SEDAR, did not agree with this position. An obvious issue was how to reconcile being "an alternative political force" with KSPI/FSPMI's declaration of support for Prabowo—although the formal declaration by KSPI/FSPMI did not come until 1 May, which was after the conference. The leaderships of some unions, particularly that of SEDAR, had openly argued that campaigning to change the leadership and politics of the KSPI should be a priority political task. This was also the position of the political group the PPR (Partai Pembebasan Rakyat; Peoples' Liberation Party), as well as of the newspaper *Arah Juang*, formally published by the political group the KPO-PRP (Kongres Politik Organisasi Perjuangan Rakyat Pekerja; Political Congress of the Working People's Organisation of Struggle), both of which were also at the conference.

Further difficulties for unification were visible in the lead up to and on May Day. There was an expectation among some conference participants that the Joint Declaration from the KGR could be launched on May Day by a united front of the participating organizations. However, it appears that a call for a united mobilization of all unions was already circulating prior to the conference by a coalition of unions called Gebrak (Gerakan Buruh Untuk Rakyat; Workers Movement for the People). On 27 April, Gebrak—which included KASBI, KPBI and other KGR participants—held a press conference indicating that it was calling for the broadest possible joint mobilization. It is not totally clear to this author, but it appears that this coalition initiative did precede the KGR conference and that key unions may have not wished to scuttle it for a new initiative that was only seven days old.

This development meant that there was not a united mobilization of the forces involved in the KGR. Gebrak included at least one union federation that it could not work with because of what was perceived to be that union's disagreement with the KGR position on LGBT rights and on democratic rights in Papua.

As a consequence, there were two coalition mobilizations on May Day by the progressive non-aligned unions—one by Gebrak and one by another quickly formed coalition, KOMITMEN (May 1 Committee for Freedom, Equality and Prosperity; Komite Mei 1 Untuk Kemerdekaan, Kestaraan dan Kesejahteraan). KOMITMEN adopted terminology from the conference. The lead unions in Gebrak[17] were KASBI and KPBI; the lead union in KOMITMEN was SEDAR.[18] Twenty-two organizations signed the Gebrak statement, including KASBI, KPBI and KSN. Seventeen organizations signed the KOMITMEN statement, with the main union involved being SEDAR.

There were differences in the nuances of the two statements; however, both asserted the necessity for the formation of an alternative political force. There was also significant overlap in the political demands of the two statements, although they were articulated in different styles. They were mostly consistent with the character of the demands raised at the KGR. Whether these two statements reflect political differences that make unification impossible is yet unclear. This will only become clear as new attempts are made to restart a process for the formation of an "alternative political force". Most participants report an overall decline in the size of the mobilizations.

On 1 August the committee tasked to organize a follow-up meeting sent an invitation to all forty-two signatories to meet again as soon as possible. Despite the divisions that emerged on

May Day, it appears that the dynamic pressing for a regrouping of this kind will continue. Being still at an early stage of its development, it is unlikely to have a significant impact on the 2019 elections. Reflecting as it does an alienation from all of the existing electoral alternatives, and therefore logically demanding efforts to establish a "third force", it must be seen as a trend relevant to medium term rather than immediate political activity.

Notes

1. KASBI is the largest of these unions, with probably 30,000–40,000 members. The other unions would be considerably smaller.
2. Max Lane, "The Politics of Wages and Indonesia's Trade Unions", *ISEAS Perspective*, no. 4/2018 (18 January 2018).
3. https://news.detik.com/berita/3946548/umumkan-capres-saat-may-day-serikat-buruh-minta-jatah-menteri; http://www.netralnews.com/news/nasional/read/136417/said.iqbal.beri.sinyal.buruh.dukung.prab.
4. https://beritalima.com/may-day-serikat-buruh-pecah-kspsi-yorris-dukung-jokowi-kspi-said-iqbal-ke-prabowo/.
5. See in particular Ian Wilson, "Jakarta: Inequality and the Poverty of Elite Pluralism", *New Mandala*, 19 April 2017.
6. http://buruh.co/deklarasi-bersama-konferensi-gerakan-rakyat-indonesia/; http://ksn.or.id/deklarasi-bersama-konferensi-gerakan-rakyat-indonesia/; https://fpbiindonesia.wordpress.com/2018/04/19/jelang-mayday-2018-organisasi-buruh-menginisiasi-lakukan-konferensi-gerakan-rakyat/; https://fbtpi.org/siaran-pers/saatnya-kaum-buruh-memimpin-gerakan-rakyat-dengan-kekuatan-politiknya-sendiri/.
7. https://www.cnnindonesia.com/gaya-hidup/20180303100532-277-280137/womens-march-di-jakarta-suarakan-8-tuntutan.
8. For the full statement in Indonesian, see https://fsedar.org/posisi/iwd-2018-pernyataan-bersama/. For an English translation, see

http://www.asia-pacific-solidarity.net/southeastasia/indonesia/
statements/2018/jointstat_womenworkersandthepeoplef_080318.
htm.

9. http://www.arahjuang.com/2018/04/29/deklarasi-bersama-
konferensi-gerakan-rakyat-indonesia/.

10. Personal communications.

11. See http://www.arahjuang.com/2018/05/04/selayang-pandang-
konferensi-gerakan-rakyat/.

12. The signatories of this declaration can be found at http://www.
arahjuang.com/2018/04/29/deklarasi-bersama-konferensi-gerakan-
rakyat-indonesia/.

13. See http://www.arahjuang.com/2018/04/29/deklarasi-bersama-
konferensi-gerakan-rakyat-indonesia/; for a published English
translation, see http://www.asia-pacific-solidarity.net/southeastasia/
indonesia/statements/2018/aj_jointdeclarationoftheindo_290418.
htm.

14. See the article by union member participants at http://www.
arahjuang.com/2018/05/04/selayang-pandang-konferensi-gerakan-
rakyat/.

15. https://www.koranperdjoeangan.com/apa-kabar-rumah-rakyat-
indonesia/.

16. Personal communications from participants.

17. The signatories to the GEBRAK can be found at http://ksn.or.id/
seruan-may-day-gerakan-buruh-untuk-rakyat-gebrak/.

18. The signatories of the KOMITMEN May Day Statement can be
found at https://fsedar.org/posisi/pernyataan-sikap-komitmenmay-
day-2018/.

Bibliography

Abu Mufakhir. "Alliances of Labour Unions as the Backbone of General Strikes in Indonesia". In *Resistance on the Continent of Labour Strategies and Initiatives of Labour Organizing in Asia*, edited by Fahmi Panimbang. Asia Monitor Resource Centre, 2017.

Ariane, Zely. "A New Wave of Workers Struggles in Indonesia". September 2012. http://www.asia-pacific-solidarity.net/asiapacific/focus/zely_anewwaveofworkersstruggle_130912.htm.

Aspinall, Edward. "Democratisation, the Working Class and the Indonesian Crisis". *Review of Indonesian and Malaysian Affairs* 33, no. 2 (1999): 1–32.

Bellefleur, Daniel, Zahra Murad, and Patrick Tangkau. "A Snapshot of Indonesian Entrepreneurship and Micro, Small, and Medium Sized Enterprise Development". USAID. https://crawford.anu.edu.au/acde/ip/pdf/lpem/2012/20120507-SMERU-Dan-Thomson-Bellefleur.pdf.

Candra, Surya. "The Indonesian Trade Union Movement a Clash of Paradigms". In *Worker Activism after Reformasi 1998: A New Phase for Indonesian Unions?*, edited by Jafar Suryomenggolo. Asia Monitor Resource Centre, 2014.

Caraway, Teri L. "Protective Repression, International Pressure, and Institutional Design: Explaining Labor Reform in Indonesia". *Studies in Comparative International Development* 39, no. 3 (2004): 28–49.

Duncan, David. " 'Out of the Factory, Onto the Streets': The Indonesian Metalworkers Union Federation (FSPMI) as a Case of Union Revitalisation in Indonesia". BA Hons. thesis, Australian National University, 2015, p. 87.

Ford, Michele. "Continuity and Change in Indonesian Labour Relations in the Habibie Interegnum". *Southeast Asian Journal of Social Science* 28, no. 2 (2000): 59–88.

———. "Economic Unionism and Labour's Poor Performance in Indonesia's 1999 and 2004 Elections". http://airaanz.econ.usyd.edu. au/papers/Ford.pdf.

———. "Learning by Doing: Trade Unions and Electoral Politics in Batam, Indonesia, 2004–2009". *South East Asia Research* 22, no. 3 (2014): 341–57.

———. *Workers and Intellectuals: NGOs, Trade Unions and the Indonesian Labour Movement.* Singapore: NUS Press/Hawai'i University Press/ KITLV, 2009.

Hadiz, Vedi. *Workers and the State in New Order Indonesia.* Routledge, 1997.

INDOC. *Workers Right to Organise.* Leiden, 1986.

Indrakusuma, Danial. "Rachmat, Tarikh (Sejarah), Hidayah dan Rekomendasi". https://www.facebook.com/notes/danial-indrakusuma/rachmat-tarikh-sejarah-hidayah-dan-rekomendasi/ 10152100952453538/.

———. "Sang Panda Api". In *Liber Amicorum 80 Tahun Joesoef Isak,* edited by Max Lane and Bonnie Triyana. ISAI, Komunitas Bambu, Perkumpulan Praxis, 2008.

Juliawan, Benny Hari. "Street-level Politics: Labour Protests in Post-authoritarian Indonesia". *Journal of Contemporary Asia* 41, no. 3 (August 2011): 349–70.

KOMITE BURUH untuk AKSI REFORMASI (KOBAR) No: 04/KOBAR/I/1998 Hal: Pernyataan Sikap dan Klarifikasi [Statement of position and clarification]. Available at https://www.library.ohio.edu/ indopubs/1998/06/25/0031.html.

Lambert, Rob. *Authoritarian State Unionism in New Order Indonesia.* Asia Research Centre, Murdoch University, 1993.

Lane, Max. "Indonesia and the Fall of Suharto: Proletarian Politics in the 'Planet of Slums' Era". *Labour and Society* (June 2010).

———. *Unfinished Nation: Indonesia before and after Suharto.* Verso, 2008.

———. *Unfinished Nation: Ingatan Revolusi, Aksi Massa dan Sejarah Indonesia.* Djaman Baroe, 2014.

———. "Worker Resistance to Exploitation in Indonesia, 1981–82". *Newsletter of International Labour Studies* no. 18 (1983).

Leclerc, Jaques. "An Ideological Problem of Indonesian Trade Unionism in the Sixties: 'Karyawan' versus 'Buruh'". *Review of Indonesian and Malayan Studies* 6, no. 1 (1972): 76–91.

Organisasi Pekerja/Buruh Di Indonesia Menurut Provinsi Tahun 2016. Ministry of Manpower.

Roosa, John. *Pretext for Mass Murder: The September 30th Movement and Suharto's Coup d'État in Indonesia.* University of Wisconsin Press, 2006.

Savarini, Amalinda. "Melawan Oligarki dan Pragmatisme Warga: Gerakan Buruh di Pilkada Kabupaten Bekasi 2017". *Indoprogress*, 1 May 2017. https://indoprogress.com/2017/05/melawan-oligarki-dan-pragmatisme-warga-gerakan-buruh-di-pilkada-kabupaten-bekasi-2017/.

Sudono, Agus. *FBSI dahulu, sekarang dan yang akan datang.* Jakarta: FBSI, 1983.

Suryomenggolo, Jafar, ed. *Kebangkitan Gerakan Buruh: Refleksi Era Reformasi.* Marjin Kiri, 2014.

Tôrnquist, Olle. "Workers in Politics: Why is Organised Labour Missing from the Democratic Movement?" *Inside Indonesia: Bulletin of the Indonesian Resources and Information Program* 86 (April–June 2006).

Warouw, Johannes Nicolaas. "Assuming Modernity: Migrant Industrial Workers in Tangerang". PhD dissertation, Australian National University, 2004. http://hdl.handle.net/1885/9954.

Wilson, Ian. "Jakarta: Inequality and the Poverty of Elite Pluralism". *New Mandala*, 19 April 2017.

INDEX

Note: Page numbers followed by "n" refer to endnotes.

ABOUT THE AUTHOR

MAX LANE has been visiting Indonesia since 1969. He is the author of *Unfinished Nation: Indonesia before and after Suharto* (2008) and *Catastrophe in Indonesia* (2010); both also published in Indonesian. He is also author of *Decentralization and Its Discontents: An Essay on Class, Political Agency and National Perspective in Indonesian Politics* (2014); *Indonesia Tidak Hadir di Bumi Manusia: Pramoedya, Sejarah dan Politik* (2017); *Indonesia and Not, Poems and Otherwise: Anecdotes Scattered* (2016); *The Urban Mass Movement in the Philippines* (1990); and *Openness, Political Discontent and Succession in Indonesia: Political Developments in Indonesia, 1989–90* (1991). He is editor of the recently published *Continuity and Change after Indonesia's Reforms: Contributions to an Ongoing Assessment* (2019). He is the translator of Pramoedya Ananta Toer's novels *This Earth of Mankind, Child of All Nations, Footseps,* and *House of Glass* and of Pramoedya's *Arok of Java* (2007) and *The Chinese in Indonesia* (2008). He is also the translator of Rendra's poems and also the play *The Struggle of the Naga Tribe* (2015). He was founding editor of the magazine *Inside Indonesia* and has written on Indonesia for the Australian Parliamentary Library as well as magazines, newspapers and edited books. He is a Senior Visiting Fellow at the ISEAS – Yusof Ishak Institute and a Visiting Lecturer in the Faculty of Social and Political Science, Gajah Mada University, Yogyakarta, Indonesia.

www.ingramcontent.com/pod-product-compliance
Lightning Source LLC
Chambersburg PA
CBHW061319220326
41599CB00026B/4952